Praise for

Are You Headed For A Retirement Crisis?

"Two concepts jumped out at me from this great little workbook: balance and common sense. These are indispensable in every sphere of life – including spirituality."

Ray L. Miller, Minister, West Olive Church of Christ

"This easy to understand and apply the book allowed me to adopt these concepts to my business and personal life immediately."

David Dickey, Owner, K9 Kindergarten, L.A., CA

"In my view, your workbook will be a handy tool for people starting in business and their adult personal life. Writing your epitaph is an excellent tool. I appreciate the opportunity to review this very helpful workbook."

Chet Ross, District Director, SCORE

"In my review of this workbook, I agree that the philosophy for success is relevant for your success whether you own a business or are climbing the corporate ladder."

Duncan Simpson, Nearing 20 years as a SCORE Counselor

"This idea that each person is their own "business" inspired me to develop my personal business plan which enables me to reach my goals."

Chris Kish, College Graduate, Returning to Grad School

"... is a must-read for anyone considering being in business. The principles and wisdom contained in this workbook are timeless. Apply them, and you will succeed."

Gerry Knode, Insurance Planning Specialist

"... has coalesced invaluable information about business and life from various sources and his personal experience. He has put it all into an easy-to-read format that can be used as an ongoing reference tool. Success or failure truly is your choice. Great job, Tom and T.J.!"

Pete Peters & Deborah Brown, The Boomer, and the Babe

"The 'Success Group,' facilitated by Tom Loegering, brings a whole new level of support services to our clients who are finding their power and beginning their new lives free from domestic abuse."

Laura Horsley, Executive Director, Eve's Place

Dear Mr. Loegering,

"On behalf of Pinnacle DECA, we would like to thank you for participating in the entrepreneurship panel at Pinnacle High School on November 19th. Our DECA members learned so much from your wisdom and experiences as entrepre- neurs. We appreciate you donating your time too, but it was a great experience to hear from entrepreneurs first-hand. Your comments about constant learning throughout life have stuck with us and inspired us to work hard in and out of school. We learned that failure is inevitable, but that it's important to fail fast and recover quickly. We also look forward to reading your workbook! Your knowledge has been an asset to us, and we hope to see you again next year for Global Entrepreneurship Week. Thank You!"

Justin Ferrara, Pinnacle DECA President, Grade 12

Inspiring and Practical – A Must-Read for Anyone Seeking Personal Growth

Are You Headed for a Retirement Crisis? by Tom Loegering is an empowering guide that takes a refreshingly practical approach to personal and professional growth. From the very first chapter, Loegering emphasizes that success isn't just about talent or luck—it's about making conscious, daily choices that move you toward your goals.

The book is packed with actionable advice, real-world examples, and thought-provoking exercises designed to help you reflect on your habits, mindset, and approach to challenges. What I found particularly valuable is the emphasis on personal accountability. Loegering doesn't just offer generic motivational quotes; he provides clear, step-by-step strategies to help you build the habits of success and avoid the pitfalls that lead to failure.

Loegering's writing style is straightforward and encouraging, making the book accessible to readers at all stages of their journey. Whether you're an aspiring entrepreneur, a student, or someone looking to make a positive change in any area of life, this book serves as a roadmap to help you take control of your future.

Overall, this workbook is a powerful reminder that our success is shaped by our daily decisions. It's an inspiring read that leaves you feeling motivated and equipped with the tools you need to succeed. Highly recommended!

Michael Yarandi, Lawyer and Future Airline Pilot

5.0 out of 5 stars
Excellent Workbook for Business and for Life!

Are You Headed for a Retirement Crisis? by Tom Loegering is an exceptional workbook that offers a unique approach to achieving personal success because in it, you learn about applying a business model to individual life goals. I found this to be an excellent perspective! Whether you're an employee or an entrepreneur, this workbook gives you practical tools to enhance your personal, mental, and financial well-being. The workbook is designed to also help you visualize towards obtaining your objectives and these are also tools that really do lead to a balanced and fulfilling life.

Having met Tom Loegering personally, I can confirm his genuine dedication to helping others succeed. I have seen his tireless efforts and dedicated support for his community. Mr. Loegering has a passion for mentorship that is also evident in his volunteer work, as he assists individuals in making personal changes necessary to reach their goals. Mr. Loegering's commitment extends far beyond the pages of his book because he actively engages with readers and mentees, providing guidance and support to ensure our progress. I am extremely impressed and thankful to know this remarkable author.

One of Tom's noteworthy initiatives is the Golf Program in Schools (GPS), which introduces golf to school students and I know that Mr. Loegering's GPS Program has helped tens of thousands of students. Through this program, Mr. Loegering imparts valuable life lessons and helps students discover scholarships and career opportunities, demonstrating his full dedication to community enrichment.

Are You Headed for a Retirement Crisis? is more than just a workbook; it's a testament to Tom Loegering's commitment to empowering others. His one on one mentorship and community involvement make this book an invaluable resource for anyone seeking personal and professional growth. I highly recommend that you get your copy today and become part of the success bound community that this exceptional author is creating.

Kandis Davis

Are You Headed For A
RETIREMENT
CRISIS?

No Savings? No Plan? No Problem...
If You Start NOW!

A Workbook for Your Success!

Tom Loegering and T.J Loegering, Jr.

Are You Headed For a Retirement Crisis?
No Savings? No Plan? No Problem... **IF YOU START NOW!**

Workbook for Success

eBook ISBN: 978-1-965761-69-4
Paperback ISBN: 978-1-965761-60-1
Ingram Spark ISBN: 978-1-965761-68-7
Library of Congress Control Number: 2025919477

Contact Tom Loegering at tom@golfps.org

Copies of this workbook can be ordered through the *successorfailure.org* website.

Images from shutterstock.com. License fees paid.

This workbook was written to provide the reader with the authors' advice and opinions on the subject matter covered. The reader accepts that the authors and the publisher are not rendering legal, accounting, or other professional services.

This workbook is dedicated to every person who wants to change their life for the better.

Net profits from the sale of this book will support **Golf Program in Schools (GPS)**, a nonprofit dedicated to introducing students—including those with special needs, such as autism—to the lifelong benefits of golf. GPS fosters social, physical, and personal growth by providing free, in-school instruction led by certified golf professionals, **opening doors to golf scholarships and career opportunities**. We are grateful to **Sun City Country Club**, our generous host, for providing students the opportunity to experience golf on a real course. Together, with your support, we can continue making a meaningful difference in the lives of young people.

GPS and Dream Centers have formed an alliance to assist their residents in moving forward from being victims of human trafficking and addiction to a productive life with the help of God by getting on their right PATH of Persistence, Achievement, Trustworthiness, and Healthy Lifestyle, by participating in the GPS Volunteer to Career Program.

successorfailure.org

Visit the *successorfailure.org* website to reenergize your success story.

On the website, you can do the following:

- **Register your book.** By registering you will be informed of updates and news. And qualify for 4 months free email mentoring.
- **Leave a testimonial** on how this book changed your life. We would love to hear from you.
- **Listen to Tom Loegering** talking to the world about his background and vision for success.
- **Order additional copies** of *Are You Headed for a Retirement Crisis?* Additional copies can also be ordered at golfps.org/store

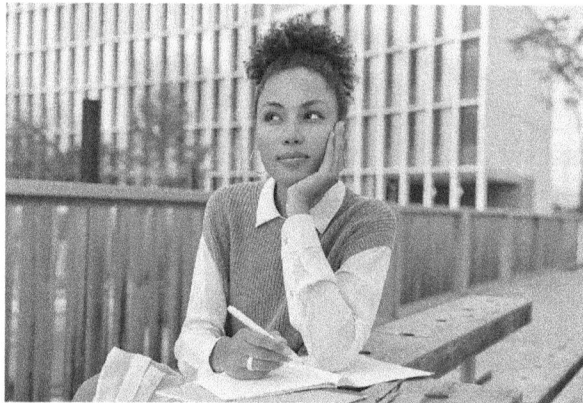

Contents

Forward

This rewritten edition of our book comes after extensive research and observations about what's needed to get the most out of our lives. After all, we only have one life to live. Life is not a dress rehearsal. We need to make the most of this one! Click your "start button" and begin your journey to a happy, healthy, and productive life. Remember, we're here to help you get on your right path so you don't retire **POOR**: a **P**erson who **O**verlooked **O**pportunity **R**egularly.

The first step on your journey is to recognize where you are now. You can't make a successful map to a destination until you know your starting point. Next, understand that the decisions you made in the past brought you to where you are now. Good or bad, these decisions have affected your mental health, physical health, and personal finances. Examining why you made poor decisions in the past can give you the insight to regain control of your life. If you discover the "why," we can help you find the "way," meaning once you find what decisions got you to where you are, applying the lessons in this book will help you find your way to a new future.

One important exercise is to begin looking at obstacles as opportunities. Know you are a business and in control of your life. To operate at a profit, you must learn to live as a productive person and business so you can do well for yourself and benefit your community.

Important definitions to help you to move forward:
Success = getting what you want
Happiness = wanting what you get.

Pursuing happiness is our goal, but as Professor Adam Grant, an organizational psychologist at Wharton, suggests, our quest for happiness might be a recipe for misery. Professor Grant believes that happiness can only be successfully pursued indirectly. It is a by-product of doing meaningful things that tell us our lives stand for something that benefits others. This makes us feel good about ourselves, which is what happiness is all about.

Do well running your life so you can do good for others.

Our goal in creating this workbook is to give you a means to organize your life, both personal and professional. Whether you work at a job or are living a dream of forming your own company, you have your own definition of success and your own personal goals and accomplishments. Yes, you can achieve success AND enjoy living your life well.

Harvard psychologist William James once said, "The greatest discovery of my generation is that a human being can alter his life by altering his attitude of mind." In my experience, this principle applies to anyone who is willing to embrace it. Success and happiness are within reach for those who actively choose to shift their mindset.

In Division 2, you'll learn how to reshape your attitude to bring balance to the seven key components of life. Remember, while 20% of life is shaped by what happens to you, the remaining 80% is determined by your attitude and how you respond. When you take control of your mindset, you take control of your life.

In reflecting on our business experiences, we realized that over the years we have adapted and changed our attitude and focus because our clients have changed their attitudes and focus. Additionally, as times change buzzwords change to match. Today you get headlines like, "How to Make a Fortune during Hyperinflation." Tomorrow it will be, "How to Survive on Unemployment," "Playing the Stock Market in a Bear Market" and "How to Make a Fortune in Real Estate Buying Foreclosures."

Your job is to change your life 20% and your attitude 80%, so adjustments are beneficial no matter what comes your way.

Everyone can agree that there are vast amounts of information available on the Internet. We've all heard the expression "knowledge is power," but beware, information is not knowledge, and knowledge itself is not power. It is the application of knowledge in an organized, well-planned manner utilizing a comprehensive written system that gives you the power to reach your goals.

A 4,000-year-old Chinese proverb says, "Give a man a fish; you feed him for a day. Teach a man to fish, and you feed him for a lifetime." The goal of this workbook is to allow you to go to the next level: *teach a person to raise fish, and you will feed the community into future generations.- TL*

Still sound simple? It actually is. If you are not as successful as you want, then maybe it is time to write your definition of success. I will walk you through creating a plan starting with your definite purpose and your why! Why are you here and what do you intend to accomplish with your life? Then you will create where you want to be in five years, ten years, and 20-50 years from now. If you are not currently satisfied, it's time to realize that you are the one in charge of your life! You will learn to think of yourself as a business on the move. You will make a plan to achieve all that you conceive.

To understand your present view about success let's consider the following "Success Strategy Quiz: What's your Approach?" gleaned from David McClelland's *Human Motivation Theory*:

> You are taking a business class and the teacher gives you the following test choices. Which kind of test would you select?
>
> 1) Very tough questions worth 50 points
> 2) Medium-tough questions worth 40 point
> 3) Easiest questions worth 30 points We will revisit your choice later in the book.

Are You Headed for a Retirement Crisis was written to assist people in organizing their personal and professional lives. We have already distributed approximately 2,000 copies of the original versions. Through surveys we conducted, we found that of all those who said they read this book, 30% made major changes in their lives! We asked the remaining 70% why they felt the book had little impact and found that they had not read the book and had not written their plan in the workbook! Don't be part of the 70%! Do the work.

Read the book through to the end before you start writing. Then come back to Division 7 and start on your journey to living life well as a productive citizen with the will and means to help others, yourself, your family, and your community.

Good luck to you and enjoy your life.

Tom Loegering, Sr.
June 2025

Authors

Tom Loegering

Tom Loegering, Sr. spent 65 years in all phases of real estate and construction business as a general contractor and Certified Property Manager (CPM). Presently, he is a volunteer doing what he loves: helping people who are ready and willing to make changes to achieve success and reach goals. He is a CPM (Lifetime Member), B1 General Contractor 1965-2018, SCORE Certified Mentor 2008-2018, member of the Peoria Chamber of Commerce Board of Directors 2012-2019, Peoria Education Foundation Board of Directors 2011-present, and V.P. Fairway 5 HOA 2006-2015, Rec. Centers of Sun City Board of Directors 2009 -2011, graduate of Leadership West class XX and annual member of the Alumni Association, member of the Goldman Sachs SB10K Cohort 14 Long Beach, Ca. 2015, BI Solutions Inc. Board member, 2015-present, and Chairman of the Board of Golf Program in Schools, Inc. 2015-present.

Tom Loegering

In 2015, Tom founded the nonprofit Golf Program in Schools, An Inclusive, Award-Winning Program that helps students find their right PATH in life, through golf! His mission is to introduce P.E. students to the valuable life lessons and lifelong benefits of golf, bring families together on the golf course, and preserve these community environmental assets. GPS aims to build student confidence, promote physical, spiritual, and mental fitness, and provide information about golf that can lead to college scholarships, launch careers, and identify the benefits of golf that can be enjoyed for a lifetime. As of 2025, over 50,000 K-12 PE students have benefited from this free, in-school, curriculum-based introduction to golf.

Tom is also the CEO of The Sun City Country Club, a family-owned country club in Sun City, AZ. His goal is to do well in business and thereby do good things for the community by bringing GPS to 950 host golf courses across the US and introducing over 19 million kids to golf each year.

Tom J. Loegering, Jr.

Thomas J. Loegering, Jr. is the owner and designated broker of Real Estate Management Services (REMS), Inc. Arizona. T.J. holds his broker's license in Arizona. He began his career in real estate in the family business nearly thirty-five years ago. He worked his way through the ranks in the California branch of REMS until 2005.

TJ expanded the family property management business into Arizona. Working exclusively in property management has given him a wealth of experience that he now shares with REMS AZ clients. Through his tireless commitment to quality service, he proves the company motto: "Good management doesn't cost, it pays!"

Tom J. Loegering, Jr.

The major client growth at REMS comes from working with individuals who wish to grow their wealth through long-term ownership of residential properties or working on real estate "flips" (residential property rehabs). T.J. prides himself on being freely accessible to clients and those interested in discussing the importance of property management in this ever-changing market.

T.J. can be reached directly at TJLoege@gmail.com.

Contributing Authors

Thad and Heather Young

There is a health crisis in America, and it's not making the headlines. The crisis of being overweight and obese is a significant factor in causing our "modern" diseases: Diabetes, Metabolic Syndrome, Hypertension, autoimmune disease, and cancer, to mention a few. Even though we live longer, we spend our later years in poor health. Like your financial life, you must invest your time creating long-term health. Creating Optimal Health is the answer.

Optimal Health is a whole new approach to well-being based on creating health with the Take Shape for Life Program. This program uses three unique components: a Health Coach, Dr. Wayne Anderson's Habits of Health Guide, and medically formulated meal replacements. These form the foundation and long-term support that can guide you along your journey. As you work toward Optimal Health, you'll learn to make choices that will help you take charge of your health for the long term. Reaching a healthy weight is just the beginning – much more is to come. Optimal Health is a journey taken one step, one habit, and one day at a time.

See Appendix D.

Sandie Sopko

I am honored and humbled to be connected with Tom Loegering's GPS (Golf Program in Schools). His published workbook, *Success or Failure - The Choice is Yours* provides incredible resources for personal growth.

Being a GPS volunteer at Sun City Country Club allows me to provide wellness resources and promote healthy lifestyle habits to enhance the game of golf.

All proceeds from the purchase of the X39 Wearable Patch will support the GPS program. Plus, exclusive savings are available for preferred customers.

Contact: Sandie Sopko 602-793-1007 (GPS Volunteer)

See Appendix E.

Acknowledgments

Thank you to my loving wife, of 50 years who went to be with Jesus on December 5, 2023, and my family for their support, encouragement, proofreading, and computer talent.

Computer-designed cover by Michelle Myers.

Religious quotes: Pastor Brandon Zastrow, COO of Dream City Church. Editing and consulting with Janet Craven, Cindy Seipel, and George Sealy.

To all my SCORE clients who asked such great questions and found the answers to move closer to their success. They have learned, and you can learn. "Success is reaching your goals; happiness is wanting the goals you reach. Wisdom comes from understanding the distinction."

George Sealy for all his computer skills and his work with the appendices.

Terry Munther – Partner on the Tom and Terry Show at www.blogtalkradio.com.

A key aspect of this rewrite is an alliance formed with Sandie Sopko and Thad and Heather Young to develop a program that encourages living your life well beyond traditional medicine. Sandie is an independent business partner with LIFEWAVE, a light technology company. This new technology stimulates the skin with low light levels, resulting in improved energy flow; supports improved exercise performance; improves strength and stamina, and overall health and well-being. The wearable patches are non-transdermal, no drugs or stimulants, and are patented. Experience restorative balance with the simplicity of a patch. Stay healthy with X39.

"Thad and Heather Young help you achieve a healthy weight, supporting your journey to better physical, mental, and financial well-being."

Fourth Edition

This rewrite and change of title continues the evolution of the concept introduced in the original, second, and third editions: **helping people find their right path to success.**

Since the third edition, the GPS program has validated our process. Not only have we introduced thousands of P.E. students to the valuable life lessons and lifelong benefits of golf, but we've also successfully revitalized a struggling golf course in the process. By gathering insights and results from previous editions, we've incorporated new information into this edition.

Of those who read this book and applied its principles:

- All reported positive outcomes and achievements.
- Victims of domestic violence shared that they will never be victimized again and have found their path to success.

Inspired by Health & Wellness Innovations

A key part of this rewrite was influenced by my alliance with Sandie Sopko, who represents LifeWave—a product that has significantly enhanced my physical well-being. Additionally, the programs led by Thad and Heather offer substantial physical and mental health benefits, reinforcing the connection between wellness and success. Their dedication to health and personal growth played a role in shaping my vision for empowering students through golf. More details can be found in Appendices D and E.

Since the last edition, GPS has also expanded its alliances—including collaborations with veteran programs and Phoenix Dream Centers, as well as broadening our homeschool and disabilities programs.

Your Journey Toward Success Begins Here

Whether you're looking to start a business or nonprofit or simply seeking self-improvement, this book is designed to get you started. It guides you through:

- Setting clear goals
- Building actionable plans
- Executing those plans
- Analyzing progress
- Making necessary adjustments
- Repeating the process for ongoing success

Is it simple? No. But when done correctly, this process can put you on the path to living a life aligned with your vision.

Why You Must Keep Reading

Chances are, you're reading this book because something in your life isn't where you want it to be. But be honest - how many times have you bought a book, read a few pages, and left it sitting on a shelf? You're not alone. The temptation to put this book aside will come. Resist it.

We're not here to sell you anything—you already own this book. What we're asking is simple: read at least the first seven divisions. Why? Because those first sections hold the foundational mindset shifts and practical tools that have helped countless others transform their lives. They're designed to build clarity, confidence, and momentum—and they just might do the same for you.

This workbook begins with an intentional twist: Division 7 comes first. Why? Because getting started is often the hardest part—and we believe action should be your first step. Division 7 is designed to jumpstart your momentum by helping you build a clear plan and define your definite purpose in life right away. The remaining divisions will deepen your understanding, but we begin with action—because success favors those who begin.

Don't Stop Three Feet from Gold

In *Think and Grow Rich*, Napoleon Hill tells the story of a prospector during the gold rush who struck gold in Colorado. Excited, he borrowed money to develop the mine. But after a short time, the vein disappeared. Discouraged, he gave up and sold his equipment.

The buyer, however, hired an engineer—who discovered that just three feet away, the gold vein continued. That mine produced millions of dollars in gold.

What's the lesson? Most people quit just before they strike gold.

This workbook is your untapped gold mine—but it takes perseverance to reap the rewards.

Your Success Starts Now

Take a moment and ask yourself:

- Do you want to secure your financial future?
- Are you looking to strengthen your marriage?
- Do you hope to rebuild relationships with your children?
- Are you striving for better physical health or peace of mind?

Now, ask yourself what these goals are worth to you.

You already have the tools to transform your life—right here in your hands. Commit to working through this book and applying its principles until you've achieved your dreams. So, let's get started NOW!

Your Journey with Us

The physical workbook, Kindle e-book, and audiobook are all moderately priced and include four months of online mentoring with the authors. Longer mentoring is available for those actively following the process and making progress.

We welcome all readers who are committed to building a happier, more productive life. To get the most out of this workbook:

- Read all seven divisions first.
- Then, grab a pen and start capturing your vision on paper.
- Enjoy the journey!

See you at the finish line.

Tom Loegering, Sr.

The Executive Decision

D ivision 7 is the final piece of the framework, where all the other divisions come together to drive actionable decision making. It's placed first in the organizational chart to highlight its role as the key decision-making hub that guides and influences everything else.

Division 7 isn't just a step in the process—it's what brings the entire framework to life. It helps tie everything together, acting as:

- – The point where all other divisions connect.
- – The factor that brings balance and cohesion to the 7 pillars of life.
- – The driving force that ensures every action aligns with your bigger goals.

By putting Division 7 first, we are demonstrating that good decisions are the foundation of success. They're the starting point for achieving personal and professional goals while keeping all areas of life in balance and moving in the right direction.

The Fundamental Question

The fundamental questions to ask yourself are, "Am I comfortable and satisfied with where my life is?" "Am I happy with my situation?" "Am I on track with my goals?" "Is there some element of my life that needs to be strengthened or improved?" "Could I do better than I have in the past?" "If I apply myself, how far can I go?"

Most of us have envisioned a better future in which we are happier and more fulfilled. We see achievement, healthier bodies, happy families, and financial security. It is fun to think about. We find comfort in that dream world. It gives us hope and peace. It helps us to deal with the daily realities of living in a stressful world. When we go to bed, we believe tomorrow will be better.

However, for many people, the tomorrows don't get better. Weeks, months, and then years go by without significant change. Obstacles continue to occur to deflect from the dreams a person wants to achieve. Some of these impediments are unforeseen and cannot be ignored. Other obstacles are self-inflicted. They are choices that people make. Either way, a person's state of being does not improve much.

Most people have areas in their lives where they could improve. The issues could be minor or major. If they are minor, then they might not be immediately addressed. Such a person is in an 'okay state' where they can live with their situation. Or they can take a long-term approach. That is, they can work on it over time.

However, many people have significant issues that cause frustration, anxiety, and pain. For example, they don't have enough money. They don't have job satisfaction. They see other people getting ahead when they know they can do better. They have bad relationships. Even more severe, some are dealing with addiction, alcoholism, or abusive partners. Such a person should undertake a more aggressive approach to changing their unhappy state.

So, where are you regarding the fundamental questions? If you are not where you want to be are you ready to change the future? Answering "yes" means you are resolved to do so.

How to Start

The first thing to realize and understand is that you are where you are because of the decisions and actions you have made in the past. Yes, unfortunate situations can arise that get people off track. However, they can be overcome by making good decisions in the future. So, once again, fundamentally, you are where you are because of you.

To begin your journey to a successful you, you are going to have to change how you think about and do things.

Let's begin with your personal mission statement, which is discussed below. It will state how you will conduct your life henceforth. You will read and embrace your mission statement every day. By changing how you do things, your decisions will be better too. You will move from the undisciplined to the purposeful. You will be more focused. The personal mission statement will act like guard rails to keep you on track to reach your definite purpose in life.

After changing how you do things, the next step is to define what you want to achieve. This book will help you do that. Goals are an essential part of achieving 'the what.' We discuss goals below.

Your Mission Statement

A mission statement is a concise statement detailing your purpose in action. Major corporations use them to align employees with company philosophy and purpose. They express 'how' a company will conduct itself moving forward.

For example, Starbucks's mission statement is *"to inspire and nurture the human spirit—one person, one cup, and one neighborhood at a time."*

Microsoft's mission statement is *"to empower every person and every organization on the planet to achieve more."*

Sir Richard Branson, the founder of The Virgin Group, has two Mission Statements, personal and professional.

—His professional statement is: *"In business, know how to be a good leader and always try to bring out the best in people. It's very simple: listen to them, trust them, believe in them, respect them, and let them have a go!"*
—His personal mission statement is: *"To have fun in [my] journey through life and learn from [my] mistakes."*

The Mission Statement for GPS is *"To introduce P.E. students to the valuable life lessons and lifelong benefits of golf, bring families together on the golf course, and preserve these community environmental assets. We aim to build student confidence, promote physical and mental fitness and provide information about golf that can lead to college scholarships, launch careers, and identify the benefits of golf that can be enjoyed for a lifetime."*

In the above mission statements, three characteristics are important for all mission statements:

—First, none of the mission statements include financial or performance elements. They don't say, "Make $100,000 in sales" or "Increase profit by 20%," for example. The focus is on the company's activities rather than the goals. Goals are important but are not part of the mission statement. Mission statements are about the 'how' and not the 'what or why.'

—Second, notice the elements of detail and granularity. Starbuck's statement stresses a single person, a single cup of coffee, and a single neighborhood. They do it every time. Microsoft emphasizes every person and every organization. Focusing on this level of detail implies excellence of process. The mission statement states that every transaction and every interaction is important. Nothing is assumed or taken for granted. Maintaining excellence is paramount.

—Third, mission statements should state what a company or person will do instead of what they won't do. The statements are positive, not negative. For example, instead of "No child will ever be forgotten," the phrase might be, "Every child is important." For example, instead of "I will never fail to analyze a deal properly," the phrase might be, "I will thoroughly analyze every potential opportunity." There is a critical difference because positivity translates directly to how a person or company conducts themselves. A positive perspective forms the elements of good decision-making. Negative statements are hollow. There is an infinity of things a person won't do. Therefore, they don't help. A mission statement should always be positive.

Now that you know what a mission statement is, it is time to write your own. You will state what kind of person you will be as you change your life. Keep in mind the three critical elements mentioned above.

Here are concepts to think about as you create it:

> Your devotion and resolve to make it happen.
> Your standard of excellence.
> Your interest, compassion, and empathy for other people.
> Your honesty with the world and yourself.
> Your regular activities that will support change.

Here are some examples of phrases that are the kind to be included. You will develop your own.

> ". . . review, organize, and plan my future every day"
> ". . . treat every person with empathy and respect."
> ". . . objectively analyze all potential alternatives."
> ". . . rigorously pursue a healthy lifestyle."

Writing down a mission statement, posting it on a wall, and reading it twice a day is a powerful instrument for making a change in your life. This action says, "This is who I am now. I live it every day. I look forward to the future. I am stronger now than ever before. I am confident of what will be."

Do this because it works.

My Mission Statement

_____

_____

_____

Your Overarching Goal

Setting goals is an essential element of success. A goal has two parts: the statement of achievement and the time frame. The statement of achievement should be measurable. Another way to state this is that a goal is a measurable achievement in a specific time frame.

The following statements sound like goals, but they are not:

> "I want to lose weight."
> "I am going to buy a house."
> "I am going to be the manager of this store."

The following statements are goals:

> "I aim to lose 10 pounds in the next six months."
> "I will own a house in this neighborhood by the time I am twenty-five years old."
> "My goal is to be the manager of this store by the end of next year."

There is a clear difference between the first and second set of statements. The second set are goals having measurable achievements with a specific target date. They are clear and precise. Progress toward achieving the goal can be tracked relative to the time frame because it is measurable. Constant feedback on progress is essential.

An 'overarching goal' is a long-term, meaningful, and lofty goal a person works toward achieving. Achieving such a goal is a vital part of a person's future.

Examples of overarching goals are:

> "My goal is to graduate college with a degree in electrical engineering." (A goal a high school student would have.)
> "My goal is to have a million dollars net worth by 40 years old." (A goal a 20-something person would have.)
> "My goal is to open my own real estate business in five years." (A goal an associate real estate agent who works for a big company would have.)

Once an overarching goal is established, it is natural to determine intermediate and near-term goals. Intermediate goals are mileposts along the way. They serve to measure progress. For example, the 20-something person might have intermediate goals of $200K net worth by age 30, $500K net worth by age 34, and $750K net worth by age 36. Near-term goals are specific things to be accomplished in the next day, week, or month. Near-term goals serve intermediate goals. In this case, it might be investing in financial instruments, making real estate deals, or other transactions that grow your net worth before it is taxed. Each step has the overarching goal in the background, driving the process.

Many years ago, my friend George had an overarching goal of moving from Pennsylvania to Arizona in three years. His intermediate goal for the first three months was to conduct financial and location research. He accomplished these goals by doing specific investigations to gather data thrice weekly. These were his near-term or immediate goals. Having this information, he determined he should accumulate an additional $100K cash to pay for the move and to augment a downpayment on a house purchase. The $100K amount translated into monthly goal amounts, which affected his lifestyle and purchases. He was very frugal during that period. The overarching goal was always present. The story concludes with his move to Arizona almost three years after setting his initial goal.

More recently, I had the goal of riding my motorcycle to all 48 states and returning by the same route in 20 days. Therefore, all 48 states were to be twice touched by my ride. It is a ride of about 20,000 miles. This is a massive accomplishment in the endurance motorcycle world, and it is called the 'Double Insanity Iron Butt Tour.' This was an overarching goal because it meant so much to me and superseded most everything else I was doing at the time. It was a goal because there was a clear statement of accomplishment and a specific period.

There were many intermediate and near-term goals to be determined and met. I needed to plan the route, how I would eat, and how I would rest. The bike would need regular service maintenance during the ride, so I had to determine where and when. I needed reliable and convenient communication channels. Many decisions were to be made before I could set off on my odyssey. I had purpose and focus. The result was that I exceeded my goal by completing the tour in 19 days.

Writing down a single overarching goal, a statement of a long term, lofty achievement within a specific time frame, is a powerful tool. It is your vision of success. Combined with your mission statement, it is a starting point for thinking positively about the future. You will be throwing out negativity and replacing it with a forward-looking perspective.

Write your definite purpose in life as your overarching goal.

_____

_____

_____

Going Forward

We believe a complete and happy person balances their seven essential pillars of life components:

> Personal
> Financial
> Family
> Physical
> Community
> Professional
> Spiritual

In this workbook we will delve into these seven pillars. You are presented with seemingly simple questions around each component to give you "ah-ha" moments that nurture determination and motivation. The questions will stimulate you to look at yourself, take thoughtful inventory, and form overarching goals to reach. Your mission statement will serve to add context as to how you do it.

Please remember that our objective is to help you find your path to living a successful, productive, and satisfying life by building a picture of your destination and then developing a plan. Remember that you won't find your destination unless you identify your location on the map. Visualize where you are and where you want to go.

I have a mantra from William H. Johnson: "If it is to be, it's up to me!" I know that developing a plan can help you realize all your goals. The Success or Failure team is here to guide, mentor, inspire, motivate, and walk with you on your journey to being and achieving all that you can conceive.

Ready, set, grow!

Definition of Success

S uccess can be considered generally, such as, "He is a successful businessman." It is recognition of a person's standing in their community, field, or endeavor. It reflects the accumulation of many good things over a period of time. It is a statement of admiration by the public.

Success can also be how a person feels about their current position in life. The dictionary defines success as an event that accomplishes its intended purpose, a state of prosperity or fame. It is subjective because it is how a person regards where they are. They can feel successful or not. Nobody else can determine it. There is no standard measurement of personal success to be found in a book. Feeling successful is one of the highlights of the human experience. That is why it is an important topic in this book.

Notice that the definition includes "accomplishes its intended purpose" This is an implied reference, meaning that goals are involved. When goals are achieved, a person feels successful. They feel good about themselves.

This brings about two other personal feelings: contentment and motivation. Contentment concerns the propensity to change or move forward from where they are. People who are not content have the inclination and motivation to move themselves to a different plane or level, while people who are content lack the impulse to do so.

So, how do these concepts relate? The specifics seem to be difficult to grasp because they are human feelings. We have 'success,' 'goals,' 'motivation,' and 'contentment.' It happens that there is a repeating cycle involving them.

Here is the cycle:

> Step 1: The person reflects on their situation and concludes it could be better.
> Step 2: The person resolves to make a change. They are no longer content; they are now motivated. Step 3: The person envisions success if they reach a new, specific state or level.
> Step 4: The person defines goals to reach the new, envisioned state. Achieving success is further defined and refined.
> Step 5: The person achieves the stated goals and feels successful and good about themselves.

The cycle begins again when the person says, "Having done that, I can do better. I know I can. I proved that I can be successful. I will move further forward." And so, we have the quote from Mia Hamm, the world-class soccer player: "Success breeds success."

The GPS Success Cycle

The definition of success for GPS was introducing all physical education (PE) students within the Phoenix Metro area to the game of golf and, through golf, instilling four core values of the game:

P-Persistence
A-Achievement
T-Trustworthiness
H-Healthy Lifestyle

We worked hard to achieve the intermediate goals of teaching students in physical education classes. So far, our program has taught over 50,000 students. We have won several community awards recognizing our contribution. We have positively impacted young people who have experienced the program.

However, as GPS has grown, we have discovered that the original definition did not adequately satisfy us. Our success motivated us to go further. It has since been modified to include all 19 million PE students in the U.S. Our model will partner with 950 golf courses to positively impact more young people.

"You can have anything you want if you want it badly enough. You can be anything you want and do anything you set out to accomplish if you hold to that desire with singleness of purpose."
—Abraham Lincoln

Finding True Happiness

After many experiences in a long life, I have found that true happiness is the desire, time, and means to help others, the surrounding community, and the world. It is a profound and rewarding experience, and the payback is manyfold.

My story —

Looking back, I was fortunate to know or think I knew what I wanted to do with my life because my father informed me at age 11 that I would soon be an adult. He told me he wanted me to consider my future and define my goals. He encouraged me to write down three occupations that appealed to me and to investigate each occupation so that I would have decided by the time I turned 12 years old.

That decision was intended to start me on a path toward an apprenticeship with the eventual goal of supporting my family and being a responsible adult. Do you know what I wrote down? A priest, a cowboy, and a carpenter! At age 12, I made my choice, a carpenter. With a goal in mind, I set my sights on being a carpenter, and by age 18, I became a journeyman carpenter! Soon after that, I entered the army, and after completing two tours, I became a general contractor at 26. That was in 1964.

While in the army, I read *Think and Grow Rich* by Napoleon Hill. Reading it helped me plan my life through the age of 40. I planned to retire with $100,000 of net worth. I planned to have my money work for me so I didn't have to work for it. There was a problem, however. I reached my goal at age 27 and retired without a purpose (other than to continue to raise my family and have fun). That didn't work well for me because although my goal was achieved, I was left with a void. Not striving or working left me feeling empty!

Even though good things happened during the first three years of my first retirement, I had no way to judge or gauge my life. I was turning 30 and thought I knew everything! My only measurement of success at that time was the money I was making, not how much I could contribute to my family, community, or country. I decided to succeed at a new goal and earn as much each year for the next ten years as I earned my whole life so far, and I would be a millionaire by age 40.

I returned to *Think and Grow Rich* and set the exact amount I wanted to earn and established a date I wanted to realize that goal. I started a business plan and began implementation that same day! The plan was handwritten on plain paper. I posted it on my bathroom mirror and read it out loud twice a day, trying to visualize myself in possession of my goals.

Looking back at those ten years, I realize it was a fun time. I was reaching my goals, traveling with my family, teaching the kids about our country's history and geography, and having a lot of fun. It was a rewarding experience to reach my goal ten months before my 40th year. We made memories that will last a lifetime!

Even with all of that, something was still missing. My definition of success began to change. I realized that I needed to set new goals. That was far better than just existing. I realized I needed to love what I was doing while producing financially, meeting my family's obligations, and participating in my community. I realized that I needed to find a "balance." I was able to understand that I was in charge of my happiness. I learned to love myself, knew all of my shortcomings and how they can be changed, and that I could alter my life by altering my attitude. I understood that following my life's plan is about the journey.

And now, my happiness is living the mission of GPS, writing and updating my book along the way, and communicating with people using mass media. It is about helping people get on their right PATH with proper values and direction. Richly refined over the years, my definition of success is living an abundant life while earning more money than we need to provide our family with love, food, clothing, and shelter. Excess is donated to causes that assist people willing to work, write their goals, and change their attitudes to reach their success levels.

I want other people to succeed as I have. Every person who does so inspires me and motivates me to do more.

—Tom Loegering, Sr.

The Seven Pillars of Life*

Footnote: *Not to be confused with *The Seven Pillars of Life* by Daniel E. Koshland, Cambridge University Press, 2010.

This book uses and refers to seven pillars of life to provide a structure for creating goals and achieving success. They are called pillars because, properly formed and structured, they provide a solid base for living a successful life.

They are as follows:

> Personal — Knowing yourself and understanding what you love to do. Financial — Handling basic living needs and growing wealth over the long term. Family — Forming solid and lasting relationships with our nearest relatives.
> Physical — Maintaining health and thereby quality of life. Community — Extending goodwill and help to nearby neighbors.
> Professional — Continuing to learn and grow to contribute meaningfully to society and achieve personal fulfillment in your work..
> Spiritual — Forming a deeper relationship with God. Connecting with a higher purpose, finding inner peace, and aligning your values with your daily actions.

Each of these pillars plays a vital role in shaping a well-rounded, purpose-driven life. When balanced effectively, they create a foundation that supports financial success, personal happiness, and meaningful relationships.

This book will guide you in assessing and strengthening each pillar, helping you create a plan that turns aspirations into tangible results. Integrating these principles into your daily routine can build a life of stability, achievement, and lasting fulfillment.

Writing Your Success Definition

Psalm 16:11 "You make known to me the path of life; in your presence there is fullness of joy; at your right hand are pleasures forevermore."

Hopefully, the personal story above will help you develop your definition of success, find the labor you love, and believe that you can have all you can conceive. Now, it's time to write down your definition of success. What would you do if you had the power to change your life? Describe what you have and what you want to be successful with the following seven pillars of your life:

1. Personal:
Jeremiah 29:11 "For I know the plans I have for you, declares the Lord, plans to prosper you and not to harm you, plans to give you hope and a future."
      What is my definite purpose in life?
      Who am I?
      What do I genuinely need to be successful? What will I be doing with my life?
      What will my epitaph be?

_____

_____

_____

2. Financial:
Mathew 6:33 "But seek first his kingdom and his rightness, and all these things will be given to you as well."
      List your assets and debt—balance sheet.
      Are you meeting your current financial needs?
      Are you growing your income and net worth?
      What do you want to be five years from now?

_____

_____

_____

3. Family:
Joshua 24:15 "But as for me and my household, we will serve the Lord."
      What are your family relationships?
      Who are the people closest to you?
      Who in your family is distant or has a strained relationship?

What do you want your family relationships to be, and how will you reach out to make good changes?

_____

_____

_____

4. Physical:

Isaiah 43:18-19- "Forget the former things; do not dwell on the past. See, I am doing a new thing !"

      What is your present physical condition?

      Do you drink alcohol, take drugs, or smoke cigarettes?

      Do you have a regular exercise program?

      Can you engage in activities suitable for your age group?

      What will you do to improve your health and condition?

_____

_____

_____

5. Community:

Galatians 6:9-10- "Let us not become weary in doing good, for at the proper time we will reap a harvest if we do not give up. Therefore, as we have an opportunity, let us do good to all people."

      Do you benefit your community?

      Do you take part in community activities?

      Are you a member of social clubs or advocacy groups?

      Do you know your elected representatives?

      Do you vote?

      How can you improve your contribution to your community?

_____

_____

_____

6. Professional:

Colossians 3:23 "Whatever you do, work at it with all your heart, as working for the Lord, not human masters."

      Are you up to date with current technologies?

      Do you know who your "thought leaders" are?

      Do you keep up with the current trends to benefit your clients?

      Do you publish articles or write books relative to your profession?

      What positive actions can you take today and in the next 30 days to be more efficient and effective?

_____

_____

_____

7. Spiritual:

James 4:8 "Come near to God and he will come near to you. Wash your hands, you sinners, and purify your hearts."

Are you at peace with your higher power?

Do you follow the values expressed by your religion?

Do you communicate or exhibit your beliefs to other people?

Do you communicate with your God?

_____

_____

_____

Serenity Prayer

"God, give us the grace to accept with serenity the things that cannot be changed, the courage to change the things which should be changed, and the wisdom to distinguish the one from the other."
—Reinhold Niebuhr

The above quote should be considered as you reach your goals. How you view your spirituality is your asset; use it wisely. I follow my God, who gave me The Jabez Prayer:

"And Jabez called on the God of Israel, saying, 'Oh, that You would bless me indeed, and enlarge my territory, that Your hand would be with me, and that You would keep me from evil, that I may not cause pain!' So, God granted him what he requested."
—1 Chronicles 4:10

It works for me, and I pray it twice a day.

Balance The Seven Parts
of Your Life

L ife is comprised of these seven essential pillars: Personal, Financial, Family, Physical, Community, Professional, and Spiritual. This workbook helps you create balance across all of them.

Let's start with the Personal pillar, as everything begins with understanding yourself.

Personal

"To know thyself is the beginning of wisdom." --Socrates

"Know thyself " is a philosophical maxim which was inscribed upon the Temple of Apollo in the ancient Greek precinct of Delphi. The best-known of the Delphic maxims, it has been quoted and analyzed by numerous authors throughout history, and has been applied in many ways. It was interpreted by Plato, who understood it to mean, broadly speaking, "know your soul". – Wikipedia, and many other sources.

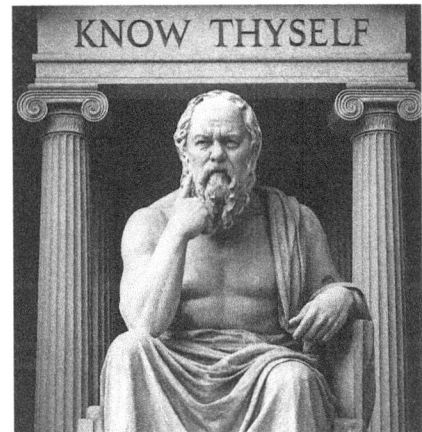

The personal part of your life is the starting point. Strong personal character is a critical pillar to realizing all you can do. It requires getting to know yourself and understanding what you love to do. It requires an honest evaluation of strengths, talents, limitations, and weaknesses. There is no greater lesson to be learned than the one about yourself.

Some questions to ask of yourself requiring honest answers:

What educational areas am I inclined toward?
Can I turn my passions into a career?
What areas can I improve upon?
How have I dealt with adversity and failure?

What skills am I naturally good at?
What limitations do I have?
How are my relationships with family and friends?
Am I honest and ethical, even when it's hard?

The more you understand yourself, the stronger and more confident you'll become. To deepen this understanding, explore books or articles on self-awareness. Self-knowledge is the first step to achieving balance and success.

"It took me years to figure out who I am, but now I'm comfortable with it. I even wrote my epitaph as a guide for how I want to live: I achieved success and happiness by helping others succeed. Success meant reaching my goals, and happiness was finding joy in the goals I achieved."
– Tom Loegering, Sr.

Think about how you'd want to be remembered. Use this as a guide to shape your personal growth and balance in life.

Financial

Having a solid financial pillar is essential to enjoying life and helping others. Money isn't anything but an enabler—a tool that allows you to achieve better things, aspire to greater goals, and enjoy the journey.

Creating a solid financial pillar should be treated like a job or a business. It is like a plant that needs water, good soil, and regular attention to grow and become strong. However, many people treat their finances haphazardly. Even professionals and upper-middle-class people like lawyers and engineers do poorly at "tending to their fields." Such people have a limited idea of their monthly budget, spend on frivolous items, and rack up significant credit card debt. Many people get by okay, but they could do so much better—and so can you.

A solid financial basis rests upon two related concepts: *income* and *wealth*.

Income is the new money flowing inward each month. For most people, this is a paycheck. For retired people, it is a Social Security check, a pension payment, or investment returns. Income pays the bills and allows a person to go to a restaurant or on a vacation. It pays the mortgage or car loan. A steady and reliable income stream is critical.

Wealth is the accumulation of assets such as property, investments, cash, or business value. Wealth represents your security net. It's what you can tap into during emergencies. Wealth can be used to accumulate more wealth. Wealth can be leveraged (used) to take advantage of opportunities. Wealth can be used to augment an income stream.

Income and wealth are both important. Income handles the present. Wealth handles the future. You want to work on both throughout your life. It takes time and energy. It is always about where you are and where you want to go. It is about setting goals and reaching them.

Improving your finances is like planting a tree. It takes time, effort, and patience. But with consistent care, it will grow strong and provide shade for years to come. Remember, every small step counts. Start Now!

You have the power to improve your financial situation. Begin today, and watch your financial pillar become the foundation for a happier, more secure life.

Family

Family can be one of life's greatest sources of love, support, and identity— whether through bonds of birth or deep friendship. While not every family looks the same, we all have the opportunity to build meaningful relationships rooted in trust and care. However it begins, family—chosen or biological—can be a foundation of strength, belonging, and lasting joy through every stage of life.

As we pursue our ambitions—whether climbing the corporate ladder, building wealth, or making a mark in the world—it is vital to stay grounded in our roots. Cherish the moments, celebrate the milestones, and accept the challenges. The thorns of family life—misunderstandings, conflicts, and struggles—are as much a part of our growth as the roses of shared victories and unconditional support.

If success could be engineered by choosing your family, you might imagine selecting parents with specific talents or achievements. Aiming to be a billionaire? Perhaps you'd choose parents who are engineers, architects, or small business owners. Dreaming of making a mark in technology? You might opt for parents who instilled in you a passion for innovation. But the reality is we don't get to pick our parents or our upbringing. What we can do is define success on our own terms, creating a life balanced between our goals and the relationships that sustain us. A written plan aligned with your values can help achieve this balance.

A Lesson Learned About Family Strength

When my children were young and deep in the sibling rivalry stage, I constantly mediated their disputes. One day, during a particularly chaotic playtime, I decided it was time for a lesson. I gathered the family and handed Michelle, my oldest daughter, a single pencil. I asked her to break it while her siblings watched. Without hesitation, she snapped it in two. Then, I handed her five pencils—one for each family member—and asked her to break them all at once. No matter how hard she tried, they wouldn't even bend.

That simple demonstration became a turning point. Michelle and everyone learned that while individual efforts can be strong, unity is unbreakable. My children still have disagreements today, but when it matters most, they come together for strength and comfort.

Family bonds are about shared blood and building trust, resilience, and a foundation of love. While you can't pick your family, you can nurture the connections that bring strength and joy to your life. You do not have to like every family member, but you have to love them!

– Tom Loegering, Sr.

Physical

You only have one body, and how you feel in that body goes a long way toward shaping your outlook on life. Being not physically fit is detrimental in two ways. First, you will not have the stamina and energy to engage in activities that improve your life. Second, it is psychologically defeating to know you do not look as good as you should.

A proper attitude can improve physical fitness and health. Once again, it is about assessing where you are and having goals to propel you to where you want to be. For most people, the formula for reaching their goals is straightforward: an appropriate diet and exercise. To be clear, it is a diet of correct food and an exercise plan with long-term benefits.

It is neither fasting nor crazy long hours on a treadmill wearing down your body. Instead, it is about embracing a lifestyle change. You will be a different person who eats responsibly and exercises regularly.

This commitment to change should be part of your mission statement. Start small by monitoring your progress. Use simple tools such as a weight scale and your belt buckle to track changes. Check your blood pressure regularly and aim to reduce your body fat percentage. By measuring your current situation objectively, you will automatically seek improvement. It's human nature—what gets measured what gets managed.

Over time, your exercise routine will naturally evolve. You will go faster and longer without thinking about it. Your food selection will become more informed as you transition from sugar, salt, fat, and processed foods to leaner, high-protein, and wholesome ingredients. This process will take some time, but it will bring long-lasting results.

One day, you will notice that you have changed. Your mind will be sharper. You will have more energy. You will solve problems more quickly. You will have a positive vision of the future. You will feel good about where you are.

So, become a different person today. Write a sentence on your mission statement. Set long-term goals. Set intermediate steps. And then decide what you will do tomorrow to meet those goals. Every step you take brings you closer to the life you want to live.

Community

Throughout your working life, being mindful of and contributing to your community is important. Not only does it benefit those around you, but it's also key to your own personal growth. I didn't fully understand the significance of community involvement until I considered retiring for the seventh time. That moment of reflection led me to rethink how I was living and what was truly important.

My wife, Suzanne, and I decided to step off the treadmill of chasing money and luxury, which had defined much of our lives. We sought a place that would allow us to live authentically and simply, where our lifestyle wouldn't be measured by the dollars in the bank but by the quality of life we could create together. That's when we discovered Sun City, Arizona.

Sun City's 50th-anniversary outreach slogan was: " An extraordinary past—a brilliant future. Retirement is worth looking forward to." This was more than just a retirement community. It was a place that invited us to be ourselves, embrace a fulfilling lifestyle, and engage in meaningful volunteer opportunities.

I contributed by running for a position on the Recreation Center of Sun City's (RCSC) board of directors. As a volunteer position, it allowed me to apply my skills and experience to benefit the community.

My goals were simple:

--Offer my services to be a valuable team member of the RCSC Board team
--Contribute to long-term planning efforts to preserve the active lifestyle we enjoyed

--Ensure that recreation center development, remodeling, and maintenance were completed on time and within budget to sustain our way of life.

I drew from my years of experience to make a meaningful impact. Some of my relevant background included:

--Eight years as a volunteer with SCORE, an organization helping small businesses succeed (www.scorephoenix.org)
--Vice President of the Fairway 5 HOA in Sun City
--Licensed B1 General Contractor in California
--CEO of Sun City Country Club
--Lifetime Member and Certified Property Manager (CPM)

"I have 65 years of real estate and management experience, which I will use to help maintain and sustain our extraordinary way of life here in Sun City. I genuinely believe written thoughts become purpose, which, in turn, leads to honorable actions that form habits. These habits shape our character and extend beyond ourselves to our families and community."

– Tom Loegering, Sr.

By giving back and becoming involved in your community, you contribute to the greater good and enrich your own life. Whether through volunteering, serving on a board, or simply being an active part of the place you call home, your impact will shape your future and those around you.

Professional

In today's fast-paced world, staying professionally on top of your game is more important than ever. With rapid communication, advancing technology, and a more interconnected world, it's crucial for people at every level to embrace change and invest in their professional development. Employers seek individuals who can get things done, accomplish tasks efficiently, and finish projects successfully.

Professionals must keep up with constant technological advancements in fields like engineering, architecture, and software development. Doctors also see innovations that can improve the quality of life and lifespan. The world today is vastly different from what it was just 20 years ago.

One major change is the rise of vocational-technical schools. Instead of traditional four-year college degrees, young people can now specialize in fields such as radiology or robotics through certification programs. These technical areas require focused training, and after completing their education, students can jump straight into well-paying careers in companies that leverage these technologies. As technology continues to evolve, these workers stay current with ongoing training and, in some fields, may need to be re-certified to keep up with the latest advancements.

In your own career, you can always start with things you can control to improve professionally:

--A positive, inquiring attitude. Stay curious and always seek to learn.
--Strengthen 'soft skills' such as communication, attention to detail, and organization.
--Understand the necessary certifications or degrees for your field.
--Follow thought leaders in your industry and stay connected with key companies.

--Read industry-specific periodicals to stay informed about the latest trends.

--Develop the ability to deliver, delegate, or discard: Be proactive in making decisions, anticipating needs, and meeting deadlines.

--Network with others in your field, especially on social media platforms.

--Attend seminars, whether online or in person, to continue learning.

--Write articles or books to share your knowledge and establish yourself as an expert.

Remember, professional improvement is an ongoing journey. Successful people are often leaders in their field because they constantly embrace new methodologies, technologies, and business methods. Companies want to hire individuals who bring energy, creativity, and innovation to their work, and it's no different for professionals like doctors, lawyers, or business owners. People tend to gravitate toward those with proven success and quality work because it makes a real difference. By committing to continuous growth and improvement, you can set yourself up for a thriving, fulfilling career in any industry.

Spiritual

Living a faith-based life is powerful. Living a faith-based life accelerates personal growth and provides the strength and resilience needed to overcome challenges. People grounded in faith possess mental fortitude, remaining calm and confident in themselves, regardless of external pressures.

Faith-based organizations like Teen Challenge and the Dream Center have proven the transformative power of spirituality, helping individuals overcome severe addiction, abuse, and trauma. People enter these programs in the worst circumstances. They have no money. They are addicted or mentally afflicted. They are at a low point in life. After going through the program and embracing God, they emerge stronger and able to deal with the pressures of life. They become productive members of society. It is a testament to the power of a spiritual life. It works for everybody who is a believer.

Humbling

For those who are not spiritually inclined, the journey to spiritual growth can begin with a simple act: humility. Humbling oneself means releasing pride, arrogance, and self-importance and embracing the idea that one has a purpose under God. It's not about living meekly but recognizing one's position in the world, prioritizing others over oneself, and being open to God's guidance.

As shared in *Jesus Is My Mulligan*, by Kent Chase, humility opens the door to transformation. It's the key to improvement and change. "Being humble" is often misconceived as a weakness, yet it's about having a modest belief in your importance and showing gratitude for being God's child.

The Bible frequently speaks about humility as a core virtue, such as in James 4:10: "Humble yourselves before the LORD, and He will lift you up." Humility doesn't make you less; it makes you stronger and more open to God's teachings.

Ideas from the Bible

The Bible is the first and best self-help book. "It is the Operating Manual for human beings created by the Manufacturer."— TL It points you in the right direction, but you are responsible for your attitude and whatever you think is honorable, right, and just. Faith is your highest power and your best option.

Parable of the Talents

This well-known parable is found in Matthew 25 and Luke 19 of the Bible. This is the International Standard Version (ISV). A 'talent' was a unit of measure. One talent of gold was equal to the typical worker's daily labor for 16.4 years.

Similarly, it is like a man going on a trip, who called his servants and turned his money over to them. To one man he gave five talents, to another two, and to another one, based on their ability. Then he went on his trip.

The one who received five talents went out at once and invested them and earned five more. In the same way, the one who had two talents earned two more. But the one who received one talent went off, dug a hole in the ground, and buried his master's money.

After a long time, the master of those servants returned and settled accounts with them. The one who had received five talents came up and brought five more talents. 'Master,' he said, 'you gave me five talents. See, I've earned five more talents.' His master told him, 'Well done, good and trustworthy servant! Since you've been trustworthy with a small amount, I'll put you in charge of a large amount. Come and share your master's joy!'

The one with two talents also came forward and said, 'Master, you gave me two talents. See, I've earned two more talents.' His master told him, 'Well done, good and trustworthy servant! Since you've been trustworthy with a small amount, I'll put you in charge of a large amount. Come and share your master's joy!'

Then the one who had received one talent came forward and said, 'Master, I knew that you were a hard man, harvesting where you haven't planted and gathering where you haven't scattered any seed. Since I was afraid, I went off and hid your talent in the ground. Here, take what's yours!'

His master answered him, 'You evil and lazy servant! So you knew that I harvested where I haven't planted and gathered where I haven't scattered any seed? Then you should've invested my money with the bankers. When I returned, I would've received my money back with interest.' Then the master said, 'Take the talent from him and give it to the man who has the ten talents, because to everyone who has something, more will be given, and he'll have more than enough. But from the person who has nothing, even what he has will be taken away from him. Throw this useless servant into the darkness outside! In that place there will be weeping and gnashing of teeth.'

It is an interesting story containing important messages. The word 'talent,' a measure of gold, is a metaphor for a person's abilities and creativity. The first two servants energetically used their 'talents' or abilities to multiply their worth. They were unafraid, and they excelled. The third servant was lazy and fearful to do more, failing the mission. The result was the first two servants were rewarded for their efforts. The third servant got thrown out to a bad place (you don't want to be that person!).

The Bible tells us to go forth energetically and use our talents and abilities to reach our goals. We should believe in ourselves without fear to realize success.

Other passages

The Bible encourages us to live with intention, to believe in our capabilities, and to pursue our goals without hesitation. Key passages such as Matthew 17:20, Philippians 4:8, and Luke 6:38 emphasize the importance of faith, integrity, and generosity. By following these principles, we align ourselves with a purpose greater than ourselves, finding spiritual and practical success.

"What you believe, you can achieve. You just need faith. If you have faith as a grain of mustard seed, it can say to this mountain: move, as nothing shall be impossible."
Matthew 17:20

"Finally, brethren, whatever is true, whatever is honorable, whatever is right, whatever is pure, whatever is lovely, whatever is of good repute, if there is any excellence and if anything is worthy of praise, let your mind dwell on these things."
Philippians 4:8

"Give, and it shall be given unto you."
Luke 6:38

"The Lord loves a cheerful giver." Paul, 2 Corinthians 9:7

These short samples from the Bible show us how to operate our spiritual and financial lives. You are in charge of your business, and life deals harshly with people who wish to be paid based on their needs rather than productivity.

Not everything in life is about making money. It is about being productive, doing what you love, and supporting your family and community. You have to give and receive. If you give bad, you get three bad in return. If you give a good, you get ten goods in return. Giving can be money or unobserved acts of kindness anonymously or with fanfare.

Balancing Golf Program in Schools

We used these seven parts of life in developing Golf Program in Schools, a 501(c)(3) nonprofit entity:

--**Personal**: One of the true joys of life is helping others. GPS was conceived to open up new vistas and expose students to opportunities they might not have experienced.

--**Financial**: GPS provided a new source of revenue for Sun City Country Club. Providing free golf to students who complete the program directly enhanced the club revenue in green fees received from the adults accompanying the students and ancillary revenue from merchandise, food, and beverage sales.

--**Family**: GPS became part of our extended family. Many like-minded people became enthusiastic volunteers. Mentoring the students creates relationships that will last a lifetime. GPS has also strengthened family relationships between students and parents by providing a shared activity in a social media-free zone.

--**Physical**: Part of the mission of GPS is to promote physical fitness. To get students off the couch, their heads out of video games, and get them outside engaging in healthy physical activity.

--**Community**: GPS offers a cost-free program to the community called Community Fun Day once a month. We believe that by making a difference in the lives of the students and their families, we are making our communities a better place to live.

--**Professional**: GPS has built its foundation as a 501(c)(3), including a Board of Directors, a formal business plan, and our policies and procedures to ensure a solid base from which to grow.

--**Spiritual**: "Do unto others as you would have them do unto you" is, in one form or another, found in every religion of the world. We have been very fortunate, and GPS is our attempt to 'pay it back/forward.' We aim to do well in our business and do good in our community!

Incorporating all seven pillars into GPS ensures that the program is not just about teaching golf—it's about transforming lives and building stronger communities grounded in faith, humility, and service to others.

How To Get Started

You are now ready to get started.

You have written your definition of Success from Division 1, and you have studied the seven parts of your life in Division 2. Now, you are ready to start your life plan.

Breaking Free From Old Habits

Change starts with breaking old routines and rigid habits. This opens your mind to new possibilities, allowing you to align your talents and beliefs with your ultimate purpose. The journey will help you achieve balance in your finances, mind, and body, and create a new, fulfilling version of yourself.

The Six Practical Steps

Adapted from Napoleon Hill's *Think and Grow Rich*, these steps are a proven method for reaching and exceeding your goals:

1. **Define Your Goal:** Fix in your mind the exact amount of money or outcome you desire.

_____

_____

_____

2. **Determine Your Sacrifice:** Decide what you will give or do to achieve this goal. Know exactly what you will give to receive that amount. Here you need to take stock of what you have to give. What experience do you have that will benefit another person or group that has the funds you need?

If you have a job, you can start by climbing the corporate ladder. Bob Iger, CEO of Disney said, "I believe that it is a better path to join a quality company, work hard and well with people, and navigate your way into the right roles than join a lower-quality company, even if you have a superior position."

No matter where you are currently employed, or even if you are still looking, remember: You will always improve your position as you improve your attitude. Develop and maintain a positive can-do attitude. No matter what your position in the company is, your attitude is the one thing over which you have complete control. Work is not hard if you love what you are doing. Getting in early or staying late will just be doing more of what you love while you develop a reputation for reliability and responsiveness. Realize, even if you have a job and you are keeping a great, positive attitude, and doing more than you get paid for, this job may not be the right fit for you if it doesn't put you on the path to Success.

Realize, even if you have a job and you are keeping a great, positive attitude, and doing more than you get paid for, this job may not be the right fit for you if it doesn't put you on the path to Success. You could have a bad boss. You might not be getting raises. Your job assignments don't lead to job progress, or you are doing work that others take credit for. In these cases, you need to make changes. Assert yourself and develop a job path that will put you on the correct career path. You don't need to be a jerk and shamelessly promote yourself or be the bad boss. Even if that works, it is only in the short run and is not the path to success.

Develop your plan to climb the corporate ladder and put yourself totally into this plan. Get all the in-house training your company will pay for. Study each of the next positions you need to climb up to – what experience is necessary, what degree is enough, and what is too much? Write a job description or acquire one from the company. Fill that position. Then contact the person in that position and see if they are willing to move up.

Become an ally and allow that person to mentor you as you both move up. You can search your company for growth or find another that has the fit, terms, culture, personality, and interests that play into your strengths. Working in a company with great people will give you better networking and offer the best opportunities for building and growth. You can easily go from a major company with strict growth patterns to a smaller, mid-size company that will give you opportunities to develop and expand.

No matter where you are now, remember that no one has as much direct control over your short or mid-term goal attain- ments as your boss. Your job is to support and promote them. If you decide there is no growth at your current company and you must move on, develop an exit strategy that allows you to keep your good relationships. Know that all business relationships are personal relationships. Network these relationships with a written plan that will allow you to achieve your goals while you work to make your boss a success and your company a success. You will grow and prosper as well. People appreciate your honest and responsive communication as you work on their behalf.

Now when it comes time to look at your own career, you can't succeed in a vacuum. Work with others that want to move up. Develop your brain trust with a small group of like-minded professionals to be your sounding board. Whatever your career path, you set your goals. You control your attitude. At this stage you decide: do you continue to climb the safe corporate ladder, or do you become the boss in your own enterprise?

What will you give to achieve your goal:

_____

_____

_____

3. Set A Deadline: You need to set a time; an exact time you want to accomplish your goal. In a year or so is not exact. May 9, 2027, is an exact date, so plug yours in now.

_____

_____

_____

4. Create a Plan: Outline clear steps and start taking action immediately.

_____

_____

_____

_____

_____

_____

5. Write It Down:

You are the boss of you. But if you elect to be the boss of your own company, find a career that has ease of entry or get licensed in the career you want to be established.

"This is what I did in my first career as a journeyman carpenter. Then I got licensed to be a B1 general contractor.

My second career after my first retirement was a real estate salesman. I put in the time to learn the business, do the best work possible for my clients, and become the office manager for my broker, promoting his company. When my broker retired, I studied and passed my broker license examination and started my third career as a Real Estate Broker. I was on my way to reaching my goals, because I was a success —because I loved what I was doing.

Psychic income (non-monetary reward) after food, clothing and shelter is more rewarding than cash. Plus, I didn't have to pay taxes on it. Helping my clients become wealthy by purchasing real estate led me to real estate ownership which helped me reach the financial part of my goals."

-Tom Loegering, Sr.

Craft a concise statement with your goal, deadline, sacrifices, and plan.

_____

_____

_____

6. Review Daily: Read your plan aloud twice a day. Visualize yourself achieving the goal and act as if it's already a reality. When you do well in the business of living your life, you can do good in your community.

Some things to keep in mind as you prepare to become wealthy: You are a business now. Your time is valuable. Start NOW!

In *The Master Key to Riches* by Napoleon Hill, you are given the 12 riches of life:

1. **A Positive Mental Attitude** - This is in your power and choice to change, adjust, and adapt.

2. **Sound Physical Health** - Your body and mind are a temple. Your duty is to keep them in as good of working order as your genes will allow.

3. **Harmony in Human Relationships** - Realize you can control the stress in your life as you apply the 80-20 rule. 80% of our stress comes from 20% of our relationships, and 80% of our happiness comes from 20% of our relationships. You have the ability to alter your attitude, to reduce stress and increase happiness in your life.

4. **Freedom from Fear** - Stress and satisfaction in life are incompatible. Develop your purpose and eliminate stress.

5. **The Hope of Achievement** - This is for people of all ages to develop your purpose, change your attitude, and realize you can achieve anything you conceive.

6. **The Capacity for Faith** - I have faith in God, faith in the future, faith that as I alter my attitude, I can live my purpose as I live well.

7. **Willingness to Share** - You can never give something away. Give good, and you receive good. Give bad, and you get bad. Check the Bible.

8. **A Labor of Love** - Because love is the most positive of human emotions. We nurture ourselves as we help others. Enjoy your work, and you will live your purpose as you live well.

9. **An Open Mind** - Receive all the known data as you form your plans.

10. **Self-Discipline** - Those who master themselves can become the master of their own destiny.

11. **The Capacity to Understand People** - If you don't take the time to understand other people you won't get to know yourself or develop the ability to know and like others.

12. **Economic Security** - You can always receive and have economic security if you produce more than you get paid for.

You are on a path to your Success! Start now to create your new reality. Your perception of where you are, compared to where you want to be will be is your current reality. And remember: You created that reality and you can change it.

Make a list of things you can change now and remove any roadblocks in the way of getting started.

_____

_____

_____

Make a list of how your life will change when you change your attitude.

_____

_____

_____

As you look at the lists, remember you created your old reality, and now can create your new one. Move your comfort zone to include your dreams and goals.

Finding Your Path:
Understanding Life as a Business

Introduction

L ife is a journey filled with choices that determine your success or failure. To navigate it effectively, we must learn to analyze our lives, correct course when necessary, eliminate what doesn't work, and nurture what does. This chapter introduces the concept of viewing life as a business—one where the ultimate profit is a fulfilling life for yourself, your family, and your community.

By understanding your life as a business, you can create a framework to ensure that every decision you make contributes to personal, financial, and communal growth. This perspective enables you to prioritize effectively, make adjustments, and invest in areas that yield lasting benefits.

Analyzing Your Life

Taking an honest look at your life is the first step to understanding what works and what doesn't.

Consider the following questions:

--What has brought you the most joy and success? Reflect on past achievements and the habits or decisions that led to them.

--What are the recurring challenges? Identify patterns that hold you back or cause stress.

--Are you aligning your actions with your core values?
Success is not just financial; it's about living harmoniously with your mission and values.

Making Corrections

Once you've analyzed your life, it's time to make corrections. This involves letting go of strategies or habits that no longer serve you and replacing them with actions that align with your goals.

--Be honest with yourself. Admit when something isn't working, whether it's a financial strategy, a relationship, or a lifestyle choice.

--Focus on growth areas. Identify aspects of your life where you've seen progress and find ways to expand on them.

--Embrace change. Recognize that growth often requires stepping outside your comfort zone.

Eliminating What Doesn't Work

Cutting out what doesn't work is essential to free up time, energy, and resources for what does. This can be difficult, but it's necessary for growth.

--Identify inefficiencies. Address areas that drain your resources, such as overspending, unhealthy habits, or toxic relationships.

--Say no to distractions. Prioritize activities that align with your goals and avoid those that don't.

--Streamline your focus. Simplify your life by concentrating on key priorities rather than spreading yourself too thin.

Growing What Works

Growth comes from nurturing the successful aspects of your life. This requires consistent effort and the willingness to invest in areas with long-term potential.

--Leverage your strengths. Build on what you do well and find ways to apply those skills to new opportunities.

--Develop a growth mindset. View challenges as opportunities to learn and improve.

--Invest in relationships. Strong personal and professional connections often yield the greatest returns.

Life as a Business

Thinking of yourself as a business is a powerful way to structure your life for success. In this model, every decision is an investment, and every action should aim to maximize returns for yourself, your family, and your community.

The Seven Pillars of Life

To live a "profitable" life, you must balance seven key areas, or "pillars" as follows:

1. **Personal Life:** Build self-awareness, set personal goals, and invest in your mental and emotional well-being.

2. **Financial Life**: Manage your finances wisely to create stability and opportunities for growth.

3. **Family Life**: Strengthen relationships and create a supportive environment for your loved ones.

4. **Physical Self**: Maintaining health through proper nutrition, exercise, and rest.

5. **Community**: Engage with and give back to your community to foster connection and purpose.

6. **Professional Life**: Pursue a career that aligns with your passions and values while providing financial stability.

7. **Spiritual Life**: Cultivate a sense of purpose and live according to your values and beliefs.

Creating Your Business Plan

As a business thrives with a well-thought-out plan, so does your life. Develop a personal business plan that outlines your vision, mission, and goals.

--Vision: Define the life you want to create. What does success look like for you?

--Mission: Identify your purpose. How will you use your skills and resources to contribute to the world?

--Goals: Set specific, measurable, achievable, relevant, and time-bound (SMART) milestones that align with your vision and mission.

Measuring Your Success

Regularly evaluate your progress to ensure you're on track.

--Review your plan. Adjust your goals and strategies as needed.

--Celebrate milestones. Acknowledge and reward your achievements.

--Learn from setbacks. Treat failures as opportunities to learn and grow by refining your approach.

Living a Profitable Life

A "profitable" life enriches not just your bank account but also your relationships, health, and sense of purpose. By applying the principles of self-analysis, correction, and growth, you can ensure that your efforts lead to lasting fulfillment. Remember, success is not just about what you achieve but also about the positive impact you have on others.

By understanding your life as a business, you take control of your destiny, creating a life that benefits yourself, your family, and your community. The choice is yours—will you invest in the life you want or settle for less? The time to act is now.

You Are A Business

Now that you've begun the journey of treating your life as a business, it's time to deepen your understanding and focus on the practical aspects of quality control and goal achievement—both essential components of sustaining and growing your "business." The mindset and strategies you adopt here will help you build a secure foundation for your future, even if retirement is a distant or challenging goal.

Your Business Mindset

The first step is adopting and maintaining a business mindset. This means approaching your life with the same discipline, focus, and adaptability that successful businesses use to thrive.

Here are some principles to guide you:

Communication is Vital

Whether in your personal or professional life, you don't operate in a vacuum. Your decisions—particularly financial ones— impact those around you. Openly discuss your goals with your spouse, partner, or close family members to ensure everyone understands your vision. This alignment builds support and avoids unnecessary conflicts.

Evaluate Your Resources

Every business starts with an inventory of its assets and liabilities. Take stock of your current financial situation, skills, time, and energy.

For instance:

--Financial Assets: Do you have savings, investments, or a budget in place?

--Skills: What abilities can you monetize or enhance for better opportunities?

--Time: How much time can you realistically dedicate to personal growth or a side business?

Answer these questions:

What are your best skills?

_____

_____

_____

What do you like to do the most?

_____

_____

_____

How can you mix the elements of both to be more successful?

_____

_____

_____

What have other people told you that you do well?

_____

_____

_____

Plan Your Cash Flow

Division 4 introduced the importance of understanding your personal resources, as in the seven pillars of life. Now, refine this by analyzing how effectively you're using your money and time. Are your expenditures aligning with your priorities?

For example:

--Reduce wasteful spending (e.g., paying only minimum credit card payments).

--Prioritize investments that yield long-term benefits, such as education or skills training.

--Create a "budget buffer" for emergencies to reduce stress and build resilience.

Do the cash flow exercise in Appendix C. Check here when complete: _____. Then answer the following four questions.

How can you make your cash flow more positive?

_____

_____

_____

Did you invest some of the money from your positive cash flow last month? _____

If not, then why not?

_____

_____

_____

If yes, how did you make your investment decision? Did you do research?

_____

_____

_____

Make Smart Financial Choices

Understand the long-term impact of your financial decisions. Paying down high-interest debt, setting aside a portion of your income for retirement, and living below your means are all critical steps. Use tools like budget apps, financial planners, or simple spreadsheets to track progress.

The Role of Quality Control

Quality control is about ensuring that your efforts consistently produce the desired results. It's an ongoing process of evaluation and improvement that applies to both your personal and professional life.

In Your Personal Life:

--Are you meeting your goals for happiness, health, and personal satisfaction?

--Are your relationships thriving, or do they need more attention?

--Are you maintaining physical and mental wellness?

In Your Professional Life:

   --Are you delivering value in your job or side business?

   --Are you building and maintaining trust with colleagues, clients, and partners?

   --Are you learning and adapting to new challenges?

Regularly evaluate your progress. Set aside time every week or month to review your goals, identify obstacles, and adjust your strategies.

What was your biggest mistake in the last month?

_____

_____

_____

What was your biggest 'win' in the last month?

_____

_____

_____

Do you feel you are making progress toward your goals?

_____

_____

_____

If not, what corrections need to be made to get back on track?

_____

_____

_____

If yes, should your goals be raised? Are they too easy? Can you do better?

_____

_____

_____

Organizing Your Business

Every successful business operates within a structured framework. For your personal "business," adopt an organizational model with the following key components. The divisions noted here are from the Organizational Chart that I run my business and life from.

Vision and Mission (Division 7)

Your vision and mission define where you want to go and why it matters. Write a clear, concise statement of what you want to achieve in life and how it aligns with your values.

_____

_____

_____

Review the mission statement you created earlier in the book. Given your new knowledge and awareness, should it be revised?

How can you enhance your mission statement?

_____

_____

_____

Communication and Human Resources (Division 1)

This involves nurturing your relationships and investing in personal development. Strong connections with family, friends, and mentors are invaluable assets.

--Consider reading Dale Carnegie's classic book, *How to Win Friends and Influence People*. It is short and can be read in a few hours.

--Read a passage from The Bible regarding treating other people fairly and honestly.

Marketing (Division 2)

Marketing yourself means networking and seeking opportunities that align with your goals. Build your personal brand by showcasing your skills, achievements, and dedication.

--Develop a presence on professional social media websites, such as Linked In.

--Always have a professional presentation in terms of neatness and grooming. Communicate professionalism with appearance.

Cash Flow (Division 3)

Make sure you have paid for essentials. This could be paying for food, clothing and shelter. As a business it is monitoring cash in, bills paid, growth, net worth gain or market share.

Operations (Division 4)

Take charge of your daily activities and responsibilities. Set routines and systems that help you stay productive and focused.

> --Make entries on a calendar of regular activities.

> --Use online calendars to send notifications of 'to dos' or meetings.

> --Stay organized, which leads to greater efficiency.

Quality Control (Division 5)

Monitor your progress and results. Are you meeting your expectations? Are you staying true to your mission and vision? If not, what changes are needed?

Sales (Division 6)

This is where you generate your "cash flow," whether financial, emotional, or personal satisfaction. Identify ways to monetize your skills and/or find fulfillment in meaningful activities.

This is the org chart used by the nonprofit that the sales from this book will benefit. Configure this chart any way you want to fit your personal path to success.

GPS Organization Chart

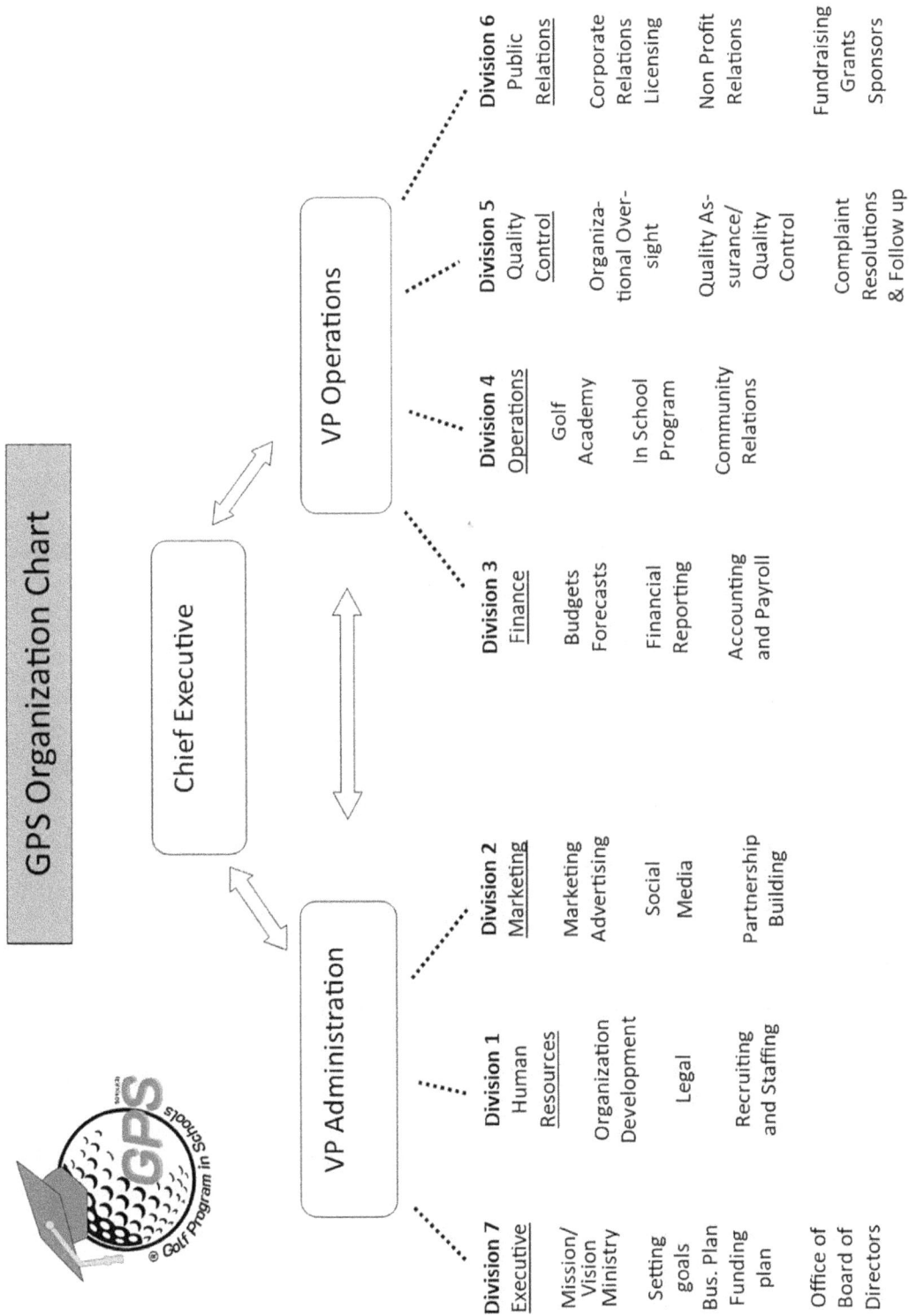

Chief Executive

VP Administration

VP Operations

Division 7
Executive

Mission/ Vision Ministry

Setting goals
Bus. Plan
Funding plan

Office of Board of Directors

Division 1
Human Resources

Organization Development

Legal

Recruiting and Staffing

Division 2
Marketing

Marketing Advertising

Social Media

Partnership Building

Division 3
Finance

Budgets Forecasts

Financial Reporting

Accounting and Payroll

Division 4
Operations

Golf Academy

In School Program

Community Relations

Division 5
Quality Control

Organizational Oversight

Quality Assurance/ Quality Control

Complaint Resolutions & Follow up

Division 6
Public Relations

Corporate Relations
Licensing

Non Profit Relations

Fundraising
Grants
Sponsors

Practical Steps for Your Business

Summarize Your Purpose. Here are specific actions:

As you progress in the "business of life," take time to revisit the seven pillars of life—personal, financial, family, physical self, community involvement, professional development, and spiritual connection. Reflect on how each of these areas aligns with the mission statement you developed earlier in this book.

Your mission statement is not just a one-time exercise; it's a dynamic guide that should grow with you. Ask yourself:

>--Are my actions in each pillar moving me closer to my purpose?

>--Is there balance among my pillars, or do I need to refocus?

This ongoing alignment between your pillars and mission statement ensures that your life's purpose remains at the forefront of your decisions. It's not about perfection; it's about progress and staying true to the vision you've set for yourself. As you implement these ideas and move closer to your goals:

Analyze Your Strengths

Identify three skills or qualities you possess that can help you succeed. Then, list three areas for improvement and create an action plan to address them.

Set Clear Goals

Identify your top three goals for the next five years. These might include paying off debt, saving a specific amount for retirement, or learning a new skill. Break each goal into smaller, actionable steps.

Overcome Barriers

Write down two significant challenges you face (e.g., lack of time, financial stress) and brainstorm strategies to address them. For example:

>--If you're short on time, consider waking up an hour earlier or delegating tasks.

>--If financial stress is a barrier, explore ways to increase your income through freelancing, part-time work, or selling unused items.

Final Thoughts

Operating your life as a business isn't just a mindset—it's a practical framework for achieving success and fulfillment.

By applying quality control principles, organizing your efforts, and continually evaluating your progress, you can overcome challenges and build a life that aligns with your goals.

Remember, your ultimate job is to prepare for and seize opportunities. With consistent effort, smart decisions, and a clear vision, you can secure your future and create a legacy of success.

"More men fail through lack of purpose than lack of talent." —Billy Sunday

Take time to refine your purpose, align your actions with your goals, and trust the process. Like any thriving business, your success depends on the strength of your foundation and your commitment to continuous improvement.

Develop Your Business Plan

To achieve the life you truly desire, you must take the reins and lead with purpose. This is where the seven pillars and your mission statement come together to create a roadmap for success. By intentionally running your life as if it were a business, you can focus on the "profit" of happiness, fulfillment, and productivity. The time has come to move beyond reflection and self-analysis—it's time to take action and create a defined plan.

Step 1: Review and Understand the Seven Pillars

The seven pillars of life—personal, financial, family, physical self, community involvement, professional development, and spiritual connection—are the foundation for a balanced and successful life. Take the next week to thoroughly review and reflect on each pillar. Ensure you completely understand their importance and how they relate to your life.

Step 2: Refine Your Mission Statement

Within the next two weeks, review and refine your mission statement. Ensure it accurately reflects your values, purpose, and vision for success. Ask yourself:

--Does this mission statement inspire me?

--Is it clear and actionable?

--Will it serve as a guiding light for my decisions and goals?

Step 3: Define Overarching Goals

Think big. Write down your overarching goals for 5, 10, and 15 years from now. These goals should reflect the "big picture" of your life. Consider the following:

--How do you see yourself in those time frames?

--How will you measure success in each of the seven pillars?

--Where will you live, work, and thrive?

Step 4: Set One-Year Goals for Each Pillar

Once you've established your long-term vision, it's time to break it down. Define one-year goals for each of the seven pillars. Make them specific, measurable, and actionable. For example:

--Personal: Read 12 books that align with your personal growth.

--Financial: Save 10% of your income this year.

--Family: Spend one evening per week engaging in quality time with loved ones.

Put these goals on your calendar and commit to reviewing your progress at the 6-month mark. Schedule a mid-year review to evaluate what's working and where adjustments are needed.

Step 5: Commit to an Annual Review

At the end of the year, conduct a thorough evaluation of your progress. Ask yourself:

--Did I achieve my one-year goals?

--Is my mission statement still relevant and inspiring?

--What course corrections or new goals should I set for the next year?

Use this annual review to create a new set of one-year goals for each of the seven pillars, ensuring continual growth and alignment with your overarching vision.

Conclusion

By reviewing the seven pillars, refining your mission statement, and creating a clear plan, you are setting yourself up for sustained success and happiness. This process empowers you to take charge, live intentionally, and enjoy the "profits" of a fulfilling life. Remember, you are the CEO of your journey—lead with confidence and purpose.

———————————————

Let's look at the Success Strategy Quiz from page vi:

You are taking a business class and the teacher gives you the following test choices. Which kind of test would you select?

1. Very tough questions worth 50 points
2. Medium-tough questions worth 40 point
3. Easiest questions worth 30 points

The test presented in the business class scenario is a metaphor for how we approach life's challenges and opportunities. Each test option reflects a different mindset toward success:

Choosing the 50-point challenge mirrors the mindset of someone who is willing to take ownership of their path, face discomfort, and grow through adversity. This is the "success by design" mindset.

Choosing the 40-point option reflects a person who is cautiously optimistic—someone who wants success but is still learning to stretch their comfort zone. This person is on the journey of expanding their comfort zone to include their dreams.

Choosing the 30-point option may indicate someone who is still operating from a place of fear, uncertainty, or a fixed mindset. We encourage these readers to reframe their thinking, recognize their agency, and begin making small, intentional changes toward a more empowered life.

Which option did you choose—and why? What does that choice say about how you currently define success? Are you playing to win, or playing not to lose?

Remember, success or failure isn't determined by the difficulty of the test—it's determined by the mindset you bring to it. The choice is always yours.

Write Your Plan: Designing the Life You Want

Your life deserves the same strategic care and attention as any successful business. That's why we encourage you to write a Personal Life Business Plan—a clear, structured blueprint for achieving your goals and living with purpose.

Like any effective business plan, your life plan should include the following essential components:

Introduction – Define Your Mission and Vision

Begin with your Vision statement— of the future you want to create. Follow this with your mission statement a short, powerful expression of your life's purpose. Define what success looks like for you personally, financially, in your family, physically, your community, professionally, and spiritually. This foundation will guide every decision you make.

Marketing – Know and Share Your Value

In business, marketing is about knowing your strengths and communicating your value. In life, it's no different. Ask yourself:

--How do I present myself to the world?

--What unique strengths or talents do I offer?

--How can I build strong relationships and networks that support my goals?

Being intentional about how you show up will help you gain support, attract opportunities, and build confidence.

Financial Management – Build a Stable Foundation

Money is a tool, not the goal. But how you manage it impacts every area of your life. Create a simple but detailed budget and savings plan that aligns with your short- and long-term goals.
Focus on:

--Prioritizing investments in your education, health, or career.

--Avoiding unnecessary debt.

--Building long-term financial security through wise planning.

Operations – Master Your Habits and Routines

Your daily actions determine your long-term results. Think of this as your life's "operations plan." Reflect on:

--How do I spend my time?

--Do my habits support or sabotage my goals?

--What routines can I develop to be more consistent and productive?

Small daily improvements lead to big life changes.

Your Life Plan in Action

This workbook includes three lined pages where you will begin building your 1-year, 5-year, and 10-year personal plans. Use what you've written in this section to draft concrete goals and timelines.

Think of these as your roadmap for the future—plans that reflect your values, leverage your strengths, and move you steadily toward your vision.

As you move forward, keep these three critical points in mind:

Clarity of Purpose

> A clear vision gives you direction and fuels your motivation. Your mission statement should be specific and meaningful.

Balance Across All Seven Pillars

> True success is holistic. Use the seven pillars to guide your planning and ensure that no area of your life is overlooked.

Commitment to Growth

> Your plan is not a one-time exercise—it's a living document. Revisit it often. Adapt as you grow. Celebrate progress and adjust when necessary.

Action Steps

> To put this plan into motion:

> *Write Your Vision and Mission Statements*
> Define your purpose and the life you want to lead. Let it reflect your values and aspirations.

> *Set SMART Goals for Each Pillar*
> For each of the seven pillars, write at least one Specific, Measurable, Achievable, Relevant, and Time-bound goal for your one-year plan.

> *Now Draft Your 1-Year, 5-Year and 10-Year Plans*
> Use the lined pages provided to set long-term goals. Where do you want to be in five years? Ten? What steps will you take to get there?

Schedule Weekly Check-ins

Build accountability. Review your goals regularly. Adjust when needed. Stay focused and honest with yourself. Remember: Success is not an accident. It's a result of planning, persistence, and purpose. Success is Your Choice! Take your first step now—write the plan that will guide you toward the life you're meant to live.

Join Our New Alumni Success Program!

Register your book at *successorfailure.org* and become an alumni member and gain access to a community committed to growth! Connect with others and work toward personal and financial success. Connect with the authors and contributors on webinars.

Coming Soon: Our Next Book on Business Success!

The next step in your journey: Learn how to start and operate a successful business. Stay tuned for details on this powerful guide that will help you turn your vision into reality!

My One Year Plan

_____

_____

_____

_____

_____

_____

_____

_____

_____

_____

_____

_____

_____

_____

_____

_____

_____

_____

_____

_____

_____

_____

_____

My Five Year Plan

My Ten Year Plan

_____

_____

_____

_____

_____

_____

_____

_____

_____

_____

_____

_____

_____

_____

_____

_____

_____

_____

_____

_____

_____

_____

_____

_____

_____

Financial Basics

Division 2, 'Balancing the Seven Parts of Your Life,' discussed the financial pillar. A solid financial pillar is essential to enabling a complete life. It cannot be ignored. This appendix presents financial fundamentals and a proper mindset, which provide a basis for success. The earlier you follow these principles, the earlier you will prosper.

You Are a Business

Step 1 is to have the mindset that you are a business. Here is what this means:

--Continually strive and look for opportunities to improve your financial situation. Examples: look for a better job, be open to investment opportunities, sell off dead weight, move to a better neighborhood, and create an Internet business.

--Exhibit discipline and take your financial future seriously. Examples: set monthly, yearly, and long-term goals. Analyze how progress is made toward those goals and the necessary corrections to achieve them.

--Follow the same processes every month, just like a business. Examples: balance the checkbook, analyze cash flow, invest money, analyze goal progress, and reflect on good and bad decisions.

--Always make financial decisions based on sound logic and research. Examples: buying a well-built, attractively priced home in a good neighborhood, investing in a stock with solid upside and earnings, and starting a business in a strong market with a solid product. Never invest substantial money in a frivolous undertaking, no matter the pressure or influence from others.

Suggestion: Make an entry on your Mission Statement that you will always follow a business-like and disciplined approach to financial decisions and processes.

Achieving Overarching Goals

Step 2 is to develop overarching goals. As we said before, an overarching goal is a lofty, long-term achievement within a specific time frame. Intermediate goals are milestones along the path to ultimate success.

A critical overarching goal is the 'comfortable retirement goal.' Specifically, the 'comfortable retirement goal' is:

By the age of 65, retire from the 40+ hour rigorous, demanding work week with sufficient income and wealth so that working in that onerous and structured format is never necessary again.

As with other overarching goals, this goal determines intermediate goals. They are: where is a person financially at ages 30, 40, 50, and 60? By age 50, a person should see the overarching goal in sight. That is, given their current situation and continuing their current processes, they should achieve the 'comfortable retirement goal.'

Achieving the 'comfortable retirement goal' will require focused effort. Social Security and pension plan payments will not be enough to offset inflation. When distributed, IRA accounts will help, but they will suffer significant tax bites.

Here are just a few quotes from various sources:

"Forty-seven percent of working households are in danger of not having enough retirement savings, according to analysis from the Center for Retirement Research at Boston College."

"A higher percentage -- 79% -- of working-age Americans believe the country 'faces a retirement crisis,' up from 67% in 2020, according to a 2024 survey from the National Institute on Retirement Security. Their largest concerns are rising costs in general, inflation, and market volatility."

"Just over half of Americans -- 55% -- have never tried to determine how much they need for retirement, according to FINRA." Financial Regulatory Authority (FINRA).

"56% of low-income working adults and 45% of middle-income working adults are in danger of a retirement shortfall, per the Center for Retirement Research at Boston College."

There are thousands of such quotes that can be found on the Internet. It takes a few seconds to find them using such search phrases as 'average retirement income.' The conclusion to be reached is that a significant portion of the population is not knowledgeable about their retirement situation, and many will have a shortfall forecasting a difficult late-stage life. Many people will have to continue to work until they cannot. Many people will continue to struggle to pay bills because of the ravages of inflation. Life will be difficult.

Suggestion: Begin implementing a plan for achieving the 'comfortable retirement goal' immediately. Be driven with the belief that you WILL arrive at retirement age in sound shape. The earlier you adopt this mindset, the easier it will be to achieve the goal.

Suggestion: Read articles about retirement planning. Get additional insights and perspectives. Understand financial investment alternatives.

Assessing Your Current Situation

Step 3 is to have a firm grasp on your monthly cash flow, which is the amount of cash coming in minus the amount of money going out. You need to know if you are cash flow positive or negative and by how much. It must be accurate and truthful. It is a waste of time to estimate expenses without a basis. It is also a waste of time to portray things better than they are. Denial of reality does not work.

To be more precise:

Monthly Cash Flow = cash in from paychecks, investments, or other sources of income Minus - cash out for mortgage payments, utilities, food, gas, and other expenses.

Every adult should know whether their monthly cash flow is positive or negative. The goal should be to increase cash flow every month. The more positive the monthly cash flow is, the stronger the monthly financial pillar will be. When monthly cash flow is positive, investments can be made to create wealth and secure the future, and long-term financial planning can begin. Monthly cash flow will further increase. That is where you want to be.

Start your financial future by analyzing your current cash flow situation. A detailed cash flow analysis exercise is provided in Appendix C, which everyone should complete. Using a spreadsheet and depending on data availability, it will take about 1-2 hours to complete.

A monthly cash flow analysis should be completed every month and saved in a spreadsheet. Much of the data will not change between months because many items like loan payments don't change or insurance only updates annually. Once the first monthly cash flow analysis is finished, subsequent monthly analyses are quickly completed.

Monthly cash flow can be increased by increasing the amount of cash coming in and/or decreasing the cash going out. You can increase the money coming in many ways, such as getting a higher-paying job, receiving income from investments, or even starting a business. Decreasing cash outlays can take many forms, such as refinancing home mortgages, eliminating bank fees, reducing high-interest credit card debt, or being smart with purchases. When a monthly cash flow analysis is completed and updated each month, it is human nature to see how it can be improved. This is precisely what you should do: look for ways to improve your financial situation.

Strong Suggestion: Do the cash flow analysis exercise in the Appendix C. It will serve you well.

The Time Value of Money

Time and the value of money are linked. Whether perceived or not, they are both part of every financial transaction. To illustrate the time value of money, consider the following questions:

> *Assuming the least possible risk, would you rather have $1000 to use immediately, OR would you rather give up $1000 to have $1020 a year from now?*

Most people would choose to have the $1000 now. Giving up the use of $1000 is not worth the additional $20 by waiting a year. There is a reasonable chance better opportunities will come along worth much more than $20.

The next question is:

> *Assuming the least possible risk, would you rather have $1000 to use immediately, OR would you instead give up $1000 to have $1500 a year from now?*

Most people would choose the second option: giving up $1000 to receive $1500 a year in the future. An additional $500 is well worth waiting for. There will be a few better opportunities to make that money next year. That is a 50% return.

Because the decision went from keeping the $1000 at one extreme to waiting for $1500 at the other extreme, there is a crossover point. It could be $1100, $1200, etc., where the answer flips from one way to the other. The exact number depends on many factors. The critical point is that the time period influenced the decision-making process.

'Time value of money' problems include five variables:

--Current money or present value (or amount), P (initial Principle) or PV (Present Value).

--Future value of money, A (final Amount) or FV (Future Value).

--Interest rate, also called the cost of money, discount rate, rate of return, or yield, depending on the context, r (interest Rate) or i (Interest rate).

--Payments, either in or out, PMT.

--Number of periods, N.

Specifying two or three variables allows one to determine the remaining one. Numerous combinations exist, and significant mathematics is involved. Usually, a financial calculator is required to solve such problems. However, the current goal is to present the general concepts.

Here is a simple example with which most people are very familiar:

Bob and Jane purchase a new car for $30,000. They trade in their old car for $10,000. The rest is to be paid with a car loan of $20,000. The question is: What are the monthly car payments given an interest rate of 6% (annualized rate) and 5 years (60 payments) to pay off the loan?

In this problem, the Present Value is $20,000, the number of periods, N, is 60, and the monthly interest rate, r, is 6% divided by 12, which is .5%. The value to be calculated is the monthly payment, PMT.

After entering this information into a financial calculator, Bob and Jane will pay $386.66 monthly. Multiplying the monthly $386.66 by 60 determines the total repayment cost of the loan: $23,199.60. Therefore, Bob and Jane will pay $3,199.60 interest over the five-year term of the loan. The actual purchase price has increased 16% (23,199.60/20,000 = 1.15998) even though it is a 6% loan.

Compounding Interest

Next, consider the opposite situation: an initial investment, PV, is made at a yearly interest rate of 5%. The amount of interest income is compounded; that is, interest earned each year is reinvested at the same interest rate. Given an initial investment of $10,000, what are the projected future values, FV, at 20, 25, and 30 years?

The answers are:

A $10,000 initial investment at a 5% annual interest rate will become $26,532.98 after 20 years.
A $10,000 initial investment at a 5% annual interest rate will become $33,863.55 after 25 years.
A $10,000 initial investment at a 5% annual interest rate will become $43,219.42 after 30 years.

Now, let's recalculate the same problem, but with an 8% interest rate. The answers are $46,609.57 (20 years), $68,484,75 (25 years), and $100,626.57 (30 years), respectively.

There is a vast difference in outcomes. The increase in interest rate from 5% to 8% more than doubled the final amount at 30 years. Notice also that for both scenarios, the final value increased more in the second five years compared to the first five years.

Here are the essential points regarding compound interest:

--The final amount will grow faster and faster with each investment year. Therefore, it is wise to invest as quickly and early in one's life as possible.

--Interest rate has a significant impact on final results. It is clear that every percentage point is impactful.

Suggestion: Learn more about 'Time Value of Money' calculations and understand how the time variable influences financial decisions. Perhaps purchase a financial calculator. Use 'Time Value of Money' calculations to analyze different investment alternatives. As a stretch exercise, look at the underlying financial mathematics, which can be easily found online.

Opportunity Cost

When an investment or a purchase is made, the opportunity to use those funds for other things is lost. The 'cost' of not taking advantage of those opportunities could be high. For example, suppose a new car is purchased for $50,000 cash. That is fine, but it also means that the $50,000 can't be used to take advantage of another opportunity. Perhaps with the proper investment, the $50,000 could easily be turned into $75,000 one year later. In this case, the opportunity cost is $25,000. Furthermore, the $25,000 profit could generate even more future returns. The opportunity cost of buying the new car becomes multiplicative.

In the corporate world, capital investment analysts incessantly look at a broad range of opportunities to direct funds for growth. Their goal is to maximize shareholder returns on the corporation's equity. By having many projects in the pipeline being evaluated, they reduce the chances for error. They pick the best few projects that meet their criteria. This means opportunity costs are not greater than the returns on the selected projects. They continue to make winning decisions.

Individuals should emulate corporate practices. Consider alternatives before plunging into significant investments or purchases. Before consuming lots of cash, allow for other downstream opportunities that could arise. Maybe hedge cash somewhat. Does this mean 'paralysis by analysis?' No. It means that one should always make logical and rational decisions before diving impulsively into decisions that can needlessly tie up valuable resources.

As previously stated, "You are a business."

Credit Cards

The final topic of this appendix concerns credit cards. They are endemic to the modern economy and lifestyle.

Most people think we would say, "Credit cards are bad." What we do say is, "Abuse of credit cards is bad." There is a big difference between the statements. People can get into financial difficulty when credit card usage is not well managed.

Here are some facts about current card usage in the United States (provided by Forbes Media):

--The standard credit card interest rate on the unpaid balance is 22-24%. This is a costly way to purchase items. For example, suppose a $1000 purchase is made with a credit card having a 23% interest rate. The purchaser pays $50 per month. It will take 26 months to pay off the balance, and the total interest will be $273.50. Thus, the total cost of the item will be $1273.50. (This is another 'Time Value of Money' calculation. Here, the calculation is solving for N, the number of payments.)

--The total US credit card debt in the fourth quarter of 2024 was $1.21 trillion.

--The average credit card balance per US consumer in the first quarter of 2025 was $7,321.

--The average interest rate on unpaid balances was 23.37% in August 2024. It will take over 10 years to pay off $10,000 in credit card debt making only minimum payments.

--In 2022, the most recent year for which data is available, consumers and businesses used credit cards to make 58.5 billion payments in the United States, totaling $5.83 trillion.

Credit card usage has exploded, and it is evident that many people are overextended. High inflation has forced people to increase credit card balances to purchase essentials such as food, gasoline, and utilities. This is a dire situation for many people. Other people are reckless with their money. They cannot resist buying the latest iPhone model, new fashion shoes, or other items. These people may never dig themselves out of the hole. The result will be a poor credit record, thus making it even more challenging to live a stress-free life. Interest rates for people with poor credit risk can be very high.

"Abuse of credit cards is bad." However, here are suggestions for productively using credit cards:

--Build your credit rating and worthiness. Having an excellent credit rating is essential to living in today's world. This means that loans, such as car loans, can be obtained at the lowest interest rates. Having "loan power" implies that money is always available for emergencies. It is a security blanket. Lenders love excellent credit-risk people. Increase credit rating by paying off credit card balances quickly or entirely. Never miss a payment and pay more than the minimum.

--Take advantage of 'cashback' credit cards. Many credit cards have 'cashback' features, in which 2-3% of purchases are credited to the account. This money can be used for statement credits or external shopping websites like Amazon.com.

--Pay monthly bills with a single 'cashback' credit card. Examples are utilities, insurance, satellite/cable TV, Internet, and telephone. This strategy has two advantages:

> 1.) Many bills are reduced to a single bill, thus saving time and handling costs, and
> 2.) 'Cashback' credits will quickly accumulate.

These bills will always be paid, so save time and get rewarded.

--Take advantage of low introductory interest rates and other offers, such as "first 18 months no interest on purchases." These offers are essentially no-interest, short-term loans. They are well-suited to automobile repairs, furniture purchases, or home maintenance projects where the outlay in cash is significant but can be handled comfortably over the offer period.

Nothing is wrong with being smart enough to finance a project over a short duration without an interest burden. Of course, the rules of the offer are to be strictly followed, such as making payments on time, etc.

The fundamental message of this appendix is that a proper financial mindset is essential to success. Having insight and making good decisions can mean far-reaching and multiplicative future rewards. Being in a good position in a few years can mean being in a better position a few more years after that. It is a building and compounding process.

Investment Basics

An important message –

Overcoming the Fear of Investing

If you've been avoiding investing, you're not alone. A 2024 survey revealed that nearly half of American adults own no investable assets. Surprisingly, this isn't always because they lack funds—it's often a mindset issue. Many people see investing as overly complicated, and given that math has never been a favorite subject for most, it's no wonder they shy away.

Psychologists call this tendency complexity aversion. It's the fear of making mistakes or looking foolish, especially when surrounded by money-savvy friends or colleagues. Yet, by putting off investing, you're missing out on one of the most potent assets available: time.

Let's look at an example. Imagine you start investing $200 a month into a retirement account with an annualized total return of 8%. If you start at age 20, your account could grow to $1.25 million by age 67. But if you wait until 30, that account would only be worth $547,000. The earlier you start, the greater the advantage of compounding growth.

Getting started is more straightforward than it seems. If your employer offers a 401(k), that's an excellent place to begin. Many plans allow you to start small and increase contributions over time. If a 401(k) isn't an option, plenty of online investment platforms with low minimum deposits help you take that first step.

The key is to start today. Every dollar you invest now is a seed for your future. Don't let complexity aversion rob you of the financial freedom you deserve. Begin with what you have, build steadily, and watch your efforts grow.

Tom Loegering

Income and Wealth

We recommend that you take as much time as necessary to study and learn about financial investments as you plan for the future. Your goals should focus on increasing income and wealth. Your real job is ensuring that your investments work as hard as you do.

Think about this: Economic statistics show that regardless of earned income, Americans spend 60% on lifestyle expenses, 30% on taxes, and 6% on insurance. This profile leaves only 4% for savings and retirement, which is insufficient to keep up with inflation. Accordingly, many Americans are in a financial rut. You must change this pattern for your long-term financial health. You must develop an effective spending and investment model that fits your situation.

We are living in the wealthiest country in the world. Colleges and universities turn out thousands of new degrees each year. However, suppose you interviewed one of these diploma holders. In that case, you might find they do not know how to develop significant cash flow for their intended lifestyle or eventual retirement. Sadly, many graduates become high-spending, low-saving people who will never take the time to understand that they are in charge of their financial planning. No, it's not easy. But then, is it easy to be poor? Is it easy to forego the benefits of your education and labor? No. It is better to learn to employ your discretionary cash and put it to work for you.

Your job is to invest wisely so your money works for you as hard as you worked for it. Growing income and wealth will give you freedom, allow you to enjoy life, and help others. This appendix presents several ideas to get you moving in the right direction. They are practical steps with proven suggestions and goals.

Here is a true story about understanding reality and taking an appropriate and better direction:

"I assisted a Christian group in developing a plan to establish a college in China. We did not want to use a traditional U.S. model that typically churns out people looking for jobs where they are only motivated to climb the corporate ladder and taught to be consumers. After meaningless purchasing, these consumers require larger houses with more storage space to accommodate all purchased items! We realized that this waste of money could be put into an investment account and earned money for retirement or used to start a business. We designed our model to teach a student to become a professional person in three years and complete a one-year internship to run a business. Upon graduation, they could manage, own, or operate their own business. Consider this model for yourself. Get the education and planning you need to operate your financial self as a business".

–Tom Loegering Sr.

As stated in Division 2, a solid financial pillar is an enabler—a prerequisite that allows you to achieve better things, aspire to more significant goals, and enjoy the journey. Finances must indeed be managed to achieve goals. It doesn't happen automatically. This appendix considers practical process steps and concepts for a brighter financial future.

Tools

Financial work requires appropriate tools; otherwise, it becomes a struggle. It involves many numbers, so handling tasks efficiently is essential. The two most basic tools are a calculator and a spreadsheet program.

A basic calculator provides a quick means to add, subtract, multiply, and divide. For example, you might want to determine how many shares of stock you can buy with your money. To do so, you would divide your money by the stock's current price to determine the number of shares.

All smartphones have a calculator as part of the basic set of features. Laptop operating systems, such as Microsoft Windows, have a basic calculator. Many people favor desktop calculators because the keys and displays are large. There are also small, portable calculators with sophisticated financial functions and operations for high-powered users who need to analyze opportunities. These are not required at the beginning,

A spreadsheet program like Microsoft Excel is essential for financial management. Spreadsheet programs are used for track- ing, calculations, and goal setting. Tracking financial transactions means you are involved in the process. That is critical for people who want to achieve goals. Spreadsheets make it easy to model complex situations involving numerous transactions across months and years. Changes to data in one area quickly and accurately are reflected in other areas. It is very powerful.

Perhaps most importantly, spreadsheets support setting and achieving financial goals. Users can create goals for the year on the spreadsheet and then track progress against those goals as the year moves along. When performance falls short of goals, corrective actions can be taken to get performance back on track. This is a critical success factor.

Spreadsheet programs work best on computer systems with sufficient screen size to see many rows and columns of data. They make it easy for the user to understand the complete picture. A few spreadsheet programs are available for mobile phones. They are tedious to use for all but the simplest of scenarios. If you are unfamiliar with spreadsheet programs, there are Microsoft Excel tutorials for beginners on the YouTube platform. Within an hour, you can learn all you need to know.

Financial Planning and Setting Goals

Assuming a positive monthly cash flow, as discussed in Appendix A, the next step is to use a portion to increase income and wealth. A good beginning rule is to allocate 50%. Specifically, 50% of the positive cash flow is used for income and wealth building, and the other 50% builds a cash reserve. A cash reserve smooths out monthly cash flow variations concerning bill paying and provides an emergency fund. As time passes, a more significant percentage of the monthly cash flow can be used for financial growth. The cash reserve will be sufficient to handle most situations. Therefore, there will be no need to grow it further.

Basic Concepts and Definitions

Portfolio

A portfolio is the complete collection of financial investments owned by a person. The plan is to grow the income and wealth of a person's portfolio.

Risk and Return

Risk and return are related. Low-risk opportunities usually have low returns, and high-risk opportunities often develop into high returns. The problem is that many people become enamored with high returns and ignore the risks involved. To build a solid financial base, it is best to begin with low-risk but sure-return opportunities. Once that is established, introduce higher return alternatives into the portfolio. The highest-risk areas should comprise the smallest part of the financial structure. That way, if those opportunities fail all is not lost. Life is not over. Life moves on to the next opportunity.

Remember: Risk is ALWAYS part of the financial equation. It must always be considered and evaluated.

Liquidity

Liquidity is the ease with which an asset can be converted into cash without affecting its value. For example, a bank account is highly liquid. One can go to an Automated Teller Machine (ATM) and receive a stack of US currency bills from the account. On the other hand, an acre of land is not as liquid. To turn an acre of land into cash requires a process that could take months, even years, to complete. One could take an equity loan on the land, but that also requires a process and time. As another example, selling a business could take a long, involved process to complete. Business assets are not very liquid.

Liquidity is a factor to consider when making investments. Not having cash readily available could mean missing opportunities. To summarize, 'High Liquidity' means the investment can be turned into cash quickly and easily. 'Low

Liquidity' means the investment can be turned into cash over a long time and with some effort. There is a complete spectrum between the two extremes.

Dividend Yield

Dividend yield, or simply yield, is the yearly dividend amount per share divided by the current share price expressed as a percentage. For example, if the total dividends paid were $5.00 and the stock's current price is $100, then the current dividend yield is 5%. It is clear that dividend yield changes by the second as the stock price fluctuates.

Yield is a means of comparing stock dividend returns. Stock prices and dividends vary greatly, so computing the yield allows comparisons to be made. Yield also enables investors to compare other investment alternatives, such as CD interest rates.

Yield varies from 0% (no dividends) to about 12%. Most dividend yields are in the 2-5% range.

Financial Investment Alternatives

Considering those rudimentary concepts, here is a list of financial alternatives with accompanying notes. It is also a practical investment progression.

Bank Savings Account

These funds are deposited in a standard bank savings account. Depositing and withdrawing funds is easy. Banks pay a small monthly interest on the balance.

--Low risk. Bank accounts are FDIC insured up to $250K.

--Highly liquid. Owners can access cash funds at any time.

--Low income. Banks apply the lowest interest rates to the account monthly.

--Wealth. Wealth is equal to the current savings account balance.

Suggestion: Use bank savings accounts to accumulate cash funds for future investments.
Typical Goal: Deposit $200 in the savings account each month.

Bank Certificates of Deposit (CD)

CDs are purchased from banks in increments of $1000, with a specific interest rate and maturity (span of completion) term. When the CD matures, the purchase price plus interest is returned. Interest rates depend on prevailing economic conditions and are stated as annual percentage rates (APR). Maturity length can be from 1 month to several years.

--Low risk. Bank accounts are FDIC insured up to $250K.

--Variable Liquidity. The CD's cash value is unavailable during the maturity term.

--Low to moderate income. CD interest rates vary every day. They will be higher than savings accounts at the time of CD purchase.

--Wealth. Wealth is equal to the purchase price of the CD.

Suggestion: Build a growing base of CDs that provide regular cash income. Stick to 6-month or 1-year CDs to make the cash value available in less than a year. When the CD matures, then another CD can be purchased for a higher amount.

Further suggestion: Purchase a 6-month CD every month. When a CD matures, buy another CD for a greater purchase amount. After the initial 6-month period, a new monthly income stream will be established.

Typical Goal: Buy a new CD on the first business day of the month.

Keep the list of CDs in a spreadsheet. Columns are: Name of Bank, Date of Purchase, Purchase Amount, APR, Date of Maturity, Expected Interest Amount (change to paid interest amount when the CD matures).

The following two investment alternatives are stock market-related. Purchasing stock market-related securities requires a brokerage account such as Charles Schwab or Fidelity Investments. There are age and deposit requirements to create an account, which vary.

Strong Suggestion: Learn the basic investing vocabulary before purchasing stock market-related securities. Read basic investment books or watch YouTube videos. You will want to understand the language of investment analysis reports. Begin watching investment TV shows such as CNBC or Bloomberg TV. Understand what the program participants are saying. Every bit of knowledge you have will help you make better decisions.

Mutual Funds, Exchange Traded Funds (ETFs), Standard & Poor's Depositary Receipt (SPDR)

These instruments are baskets of stocks with a common theme, such as high technology, pharmaceuticals, income, and growth. Some of these funds emulate stock market performance. There are many varieties. An investor buys shares in the fund rather than the individual stocks. A fund management team usually charges a supervision fee, which is paid from fund performance.

--Low to moderate risk. Because the fund includes numerous stocks, the risk is spread out among them. That said, macroeconomic events could affect all the funds' stocks. For example, the US could enact new regulations on pharmaceutical companies that adversely affect all companies in a pharmaceutical-oriented fund.

--Liquidity. Fund stocks are readily sold on stock markets.

--Income. Income varies significantly from one fund to another. Some funds pay no distributions. Others pay regular amounts, even monthly. Income distributions are part of the research process.

--Wealth. Funds with expert management will have a positive track record, increasing the owner's wealth over time as the price of the fund's stock increases. Usually, purchasing funds is a long-term investment option. Every fund has stocks that do well and others that do not. The fund's performance is an average of the stocks' performances in the fund. Purchasers of funds are investing in the fund's general growth concept, which is realized over a long period.

Suggestion: Purchasing a few managed funds is a good place to start in stock market-related investing. The investor is relying on the expertise of fund managers to achieve performance. Risk is usually low. Investors should do research to determine funds with a good track record. There are many resources available.

Typical goal: Do research on funds over the next month. Then, purchase the best-looking candidate.

Individual Stocks

Stocks represent ownership in a publicly traded company. Stockholders get to vote in the annual shareholders meeting and qualify for declared dividends.

--Risk varies greatly from low to high. Utility companies are low-risk because they have a steady income stream. Start-up high-tech companies are high-risk because they will have negative cash flow in the early years. Investors should constantly evaluate risk versus return.

--Liquidity. Individual stocks are easily sold on stock markets.

--Income. Varies greatly. Many companies distribute dividends every quarter. They also grow their dividends. Other companies do not declare dividends; they reinvest their cash into growth.

--Wealth. Stock prices (and therefore wealth) can increase 10 times and even 100 times the original amount quickly. Creating wealthy portfolios is the major attractiveness of buying stocks.

Suggestion: Research industry segments (such as utilities, healthcare, technology, etc.) before purchasing a stock. Learn who the industry leaders are. Read analyst reports on each leading company. Become acquainted with why certain companies have a better upside than others. An informed investor is a good investor.

Further suggestion: Once a stock is selected for purchase, do so over some time. That is, accumulate the stock rather than diving in entirely at first. This will average the investment price per share.

Typical vision: Purchase shares at the beginning of every month. Accumulate wealth with smart, informed investments. Create income by investing in stocks with high dividend yields and yearly growth.

Future

As the portfolio is built, continue to look for additional opportunities. Become a savvy, mature investor looking for tax and macroeconomic trends that can magnify wealth to extraordinary levels.

Monthly Cash Flow Analysis Exercise

Most people want to retire comfortably, but very few take the necessary steps to make it happen or understand the process. The truth is, financial stability isn't built on luck or income level; it's built on consistent habits, and the most powerful of those is understanding your monthly cash flow. This isn't just budgeting, it's taking control of your financial life by knowing exactly what comes in, what goes out, and what's left to grow your future. Yes, it takes effort. But once you see how small shifts in your awareness lead to significant changes in your confidence and long-term security, you'll wonder why you didn't start sooner.

Analyzing monthly cash flow is an essential activity for financial success. The goal is to determine how many funds are available for investment at the end of the month. Knowing that amount determines the financial decisions to be made.

As you will see, monthly cash flow analysis is not the same as balancing a checkbook at the end of the month and determining how much cash is available. One key difference is that amounts are expressed in terms of monthly values. For example, property taxes are usually paid once a year. For the monthly cash flow analysis, the yearly property tax amount is divided by 12 and appears as such in the spreadsheet. As another example, people paid every other week (every 14 days) make 1.07 (30 divided by 28) times the total of the 4-week take-home payment amount. Interest from a six-month Certificate of Deposit (CD) is divided by 6.

A spreadsheet program is necessary for this exercise. It should be saved monthly for future reference. Below is a list of the major sections of the spreadsheet. It is followed with a detailed commentary on each section, which gives you clear direction on how to proceed.

> Section A. List of Cash Income Sources and Amounts.
> Section B. List of Recurring Basic Monthly Expenses.
> Section C. Calculation of Basic Living Cash Flow Margin (Section A total – minus Section B total).
> Section D. Detailed List of Actual Food Expenses for the Month.
> Section E. Detailed List of Gasoline Expenses for the Month.
> Section F. Detailed List of Other Monthly Expenses (not included in Section B).
> Section G. Monthly Cash Flow Margin (subtract Sections D, E, and F totals from Section C)

Section A – List of Cash Income Sources and Amounts

Section A lists the cash coming for the month. Here are some of the possible items:

--Paycheck. Use the cash payment amount deposited in the bank. If paychecks are issued every two weeks, multiply the cash amount by 1.07 to put it on a 30-day basis. To be clear, this is the amount after ALL deductions have been made, such as withholding taxes and Social Security.

--Social Security. Use the monthly cash payment amount.

--Pension Payments. Use the monthly cash payment amount.

--Dividends, cash payment -- Dividends are usually paid on a quarterly basis. They can be forecasted accurately once the dividend is declared. Divide quarterly cash dividends by 3 to put them on a monthly basis.

--Certificate of Deposit Interest – Payments are usually made in lump sums when the CD matures. The amount can be accurately estimated when the CD is purchased. CDs vary in length from 1 month to several years. Divide the estimated cash interest by the number of months until the CD matures.

--Other monthly cash payments – Other amounts are possible such as rent payments, royalty payments, and settlements. Adjust them to monthly values as appropriate.

Single, good fortune amounts – Every so often, people receive cash checks because of some unusual circumstance. For example, in 2020, the US Treasury issued COVID-19 checks to assist people weathering the pandemic. Such checks SHOULD NOT be included in the analysis. The purpose of the analysis is to get an understanding of the regular monthly

	Monthly Cash Flow Analysis Exercise	
1	Monthly Cash Flow Analysis Exercise	
2		
3		Amount ($)
4	A. Cash Income	
5	Paycheck	5000.00
6	Interest, various	100.00
7		
8		
9	Total	5100.00
10		

situation. Including such checks would present a false picture of reality.

Using the spreadsheet, here is a typical Section A example. The investor's name is Robert.
In this example, Robert's monthly take-home paycheck amount is $5000. This is the amount after all deductions have been made. It is the amount deposited in the bank. Robert also earns monthly interest of about $100 from various sources. His monthly cash intake is $5100.

Section B. List of Recurring Basic Monthly Expenses

Section B lists the regular cash going out for the month. It doesn't include one-time purchases, such as car repairs and doctor bills. The idea is to capture standard and regular expenses. Many items are the same from month to month. Here are some of the possible items:

--Mortgage or rent payments.

--Car loan payment

--Property Taxes. #

--Energy bills: average electric, natural gas, or oil amounts. *

--Telephone bill.

--Entertainment Media bills, such as Internet, streaming, cable, or satellite.

--Average food expenditures. *

--Average gasoline expenditures. *

--Insurance payments: medical, car and house. #

--Any other recurring monthly charges

--Income Taxes. People on a salary will have income taxes deducted from their paychecks. If additional taxes were paid at filing in the last year, then divide that amount by 12 and add it to the current recurring expenses. If there is a refund, do the same, but the number will be negative. Retired people often file quarterly tax payments, which can be restated on a monthly basis.

Average values should be determined from the past 12 months' records. It might be necessary to estimate these values initially and then gather data in the future. Adjust per month.
 # Property taxes and insurance payments are often made on a 6-month or 12-month basis. Convert to monthly amounts. For example, a 12- month (or yearly) payment would be divided by 12.

Using the spreadsheet, here is a typical Section B example. Robert's monthly expenses are mostly self-explanatory. Robert had a tax refund of $600. This translates to a monthly negative amount of $50 (because it is a negative expense). Robert's recurring monthly expenses total to $2990.

11	B. Recurring Expenses	
12	Rent	1500.00
13	Car Loan	500.00
14	Electric Bill	125.00
15	Telephone	60.00
16	Internet	80.00
17	Insurance	250.00
18	Avg Food	350.00
19	Avg Gasoline	175.00
20		
21	Income Taxes	-50.00
22		
23	Total	2990.00

Section C. Calculation of Basic Living Cash Flow Margin
(Section A total minus Section B total)

Section C is a one-line entry, which is the Section A total minus the Section B total. This value is the 'Basic Living Cash Flow Margin.' This is a very important number because it indicates fundamental cash flow health. If the value is positive, it means that fundamental household operating expenses are being covered by regular and repeatable cash income. If this number is negative, then fundamental household finances are unsound. Each month, the household is sinking further and further into debt. Significant action is necessary to right the ship.

Here is a summary of the spreadsheet, including Section C.

Robert's Basic Living Cash Flow Margin is $2110. This shows that his basic cash flow is okay. He has $2110 per month to handle extra expenses and make investments.

		Amount ($)
1	Monthly Cash Flow Analysis Exercise	
2		
3		Amount ($)
4	A. Cash Income	
5	Paycheck	5000.00
6	Interest, various	100.00
7		
8		
9	Total	5100.00
10		
11	B. Recurring Expenses	
12	Rent	1500.00
13	Car Loan	500.00
14	Electric Bill	125.00
15	Telephone	60.00
16	Internet	80.00
17	Insurance	250.00
18	Avg Food	350.00
19	Avg Gasoline	175.00
20		
21	Income Taxes	-50.00
22		
23	Total	2990.00
24		
25	C. Basic Living Cash Flow Margin	2110.00

Section D. Detailed List of Actual Food Expenses for the Month

Section D is a listing of all food expenses for the month. Receipts from the grocery store are used to make entries. Section D will be used to determine monthly food averages. One possible strategy is to use a particular credit card for only and all grocery purchases. Then use the monthly credit card statement to make entries into the spreadsheet.

The last lines of Section D compare the actual monthly total with the estimated amount in Section B. The difference, positive or negative, is computed on the last line. This amount has two purposes: 1.) use as an indicator to modify the average value in Section B, and 2.) used to compute the final cash flow for the month. For example, if the difference is significantly positive, it indicates the value in Section B should be increased, thereby reducing the 'Basic Living Cash Flow Margin.' The opposite is true if the value is negative.

Section E. Detailed List of Gasoline Expenses for the Month

Section E is a listing of all gasoline expenses for the month. Receipts from the gasoline station are used to make entries. Section E will be used to determine monthly averages. Again, one possible strategy is to use a particular credit card for only and all gasoline purchases. Then use the monthly credit card statement to make entries into the spreadsheet. The last lines of Section E have the same meaning as the last lines in Section D.

Here are Sections D and E.

In the interest of saving space, the individual food and gasoline expenses are not shown. You should list each individual food and gasoline transaction. The easiest thing to do is get receipts at the grocery store and gasoline station. Every so often enter them into the spreadsheet.

Robert spent $375 on food during the month, which is $25 above his average. He also spent $140 on gasoline, which is $35 below his average.

27			
28	D. Detailed Food Expenses		
29	Several items		375.00
30			
31	Total		375.00
32	Difference From Avg		25.00
33			
34			
35	E. Detailed Gasoline Expenses		
36	Several items		140.00
37			
38	Total		140.00
39	Difference from Avg		-35.00
40			

Section F. Detailed List of Other Monthly Expenses

This spreadsheet section itemizes non-regular purchases and credit card payments made during the month. It includes doctor bills, payments to contractors for services rendered, pet medical services, gifts, clothing, Amazon purchases, event tickets, and anything purchased on a one-time, special item basis. If something was purchased on a credit card, the credit card pay- ment is entered as opposed to the initial amount.

For example, suppose a Discover Card was used to purchase a new camera for $400 using a no-interest Discover Card special offer. The purchaser pays $100 per month for 4 months. Then, $100 will be entered in Section F, not $400.

This month, Robert had additional expenses of $650. He made payments to two credit cards and paid a doctor's bill of $300.

41			
42	F. Other Expenses		
43	Credit Card #1	200.00	
44	Credit Card #2	150.00	
45	Doctor	300.00	
46			
47			
48	Total	650.00	

Section G. Monthly Cash Flow Margin for the Month

This section computes the complete monthly cash flow margin.
It is Section C amount

> --minus the over/under amount from Section D
> --minus the over/under amount from Section E
> --minus the total from Section F

If the Section G amount is positive, all bills have been paid for the month, and there is a surplus of cash. If the Section G amount is negative, all liabilities have not been handled that month. In that case, the next appropriate actions should be taken. Perhaps it is a temporary situation, or perhaps it is indicative of more serious issues. In either case, you will know much more about your financial situation.

Sections D (difference from average), E (difference from average), and F are subtracted from the value in Section C. With all cash transactions considered, Robert's Monthly Cash Flow Margin is $1470.

We recommend that Robert invest 50% of the $1470, which is $735. The remainder is to be used for cash surplus buildup. By investing $735 monthly, Robert's Monthly Cash Flow Margin will increase. With the right investment strategy, he could invest $800 monthly the following year, then $900, and so on. This plan means Robert will continue to increase his income and wealth, which is exactly what he should do.

25	**C. Basic Living Cash Flow Margin**	**2110.00**
26		
27		
28	D. Detailed Food Expenses	
29	Several items	375.00
30		
31	Total	375.00
32	Difference From Avg	25.00
33		
34		
35	E. Detailed Gasoline Expenses	
36	Several items	140.00
37		
38	Total	140.00
39	Difference from Avg	-35.00
40		
41		
42	F. Other Expenses	
43	Credit Card #1	200.00
44	Credit Card #2	150.00
45	Doctor	300.00
46		
47		
48	Total	650.00
49		
50	**G. Monthly Cash Flow Margin**	**1470.00**
51		

Achieving Optimal Health

If you could achieve optimal health, would you want it? If you said yes…great. And I'm sorry to say, desire alone is not enough. There are over 30,000 diets on the market. People spend millions on gyms, and still, we fail to achieve our health goals 85% of the time.

While most people have the desire, they often lack the correct theory and proper method to achieve and sustain the vibrant health that they crave.

Desire + Correct Theory + Proper Method = Predictable Transformation

The good news is that transforming your life and creating optimal health is possible. Our program was created by Dr. Wayne Andersen and is presented in his book Habits of Health—The Path to Permanent Weight Control and Optimal Health.

We help people achieve extraordinary results. By coaching people to Optimal Health by changing their poor habits into healthy ones, we help our clients achieve their dreams and reach their potential. It all starts with getting in touch with your "WHY." Why do you want better health, to lose weight, and to live an abundant and healthy life? We use the STOP, CHALLENGE, CHOOSE system to help you achieve the healthy life you desire.

STOP

We want you to stop, take a deep breath, and momentarily silence the chaos. Jump off that hamster wheel. Close the door to your office. Take off the electronic leash. Put the kids to bed. Put your headset on and play some nice background music. Switch your devices to airplane mode.

One of the key elements of STOP, CHALLENGE, CHOOSE is finding ways to slow down and pay attention to where you are right now. It's an essential first step on your journey to a better, healthier life because it can help you rediscover yourself and what matters to you.

CHALLENGE

Ask yourself: Are you making the choices that are leading toward health? We know that eating right will improve our health, yet, in the moment we can't help but grab the cheeseburger or eat the sugary doughnuts. One doughnut can't really lead to obesity or diabetes, can it? We know we should be more physically active, but our favorite TV show is on.

When we coach our clients, we use a Well-Being Evaluation that includes Physical Health, Mental Health and Financial Health. Our well-being is a great measure of our quality of life. If it needs improvement and you want to take action, we can help.

If you have been operating mindlessly and have allowed your short-term desires to dictate your daily lifestyle, we can help you choose a different path. One that will build for you the currency of life that matters and allow you to thrive in what is most important to you.

Optimal Health is really about organizing your life around the key areas we have identified, empowering you to create well-being, and ensuring that your daily choices support those long-term objectives.

CHOOSE

This fundamental decision to improve your health and your life will immediately change the initial conditions in everything you do. The fantastic part is that as you improve in each area, even in small ways, the other areas of your life will also be affected, advancing your overall well-being. Similar to the butterfly effect, the simplest increase in positive choices combined with the decrease in negative choices will trigger a chain of events that will help you transform your health and your life.

CREATE HEALTH AND TRANSFORM YOUR LIFE

Take Shape For Life is a whole new approach to well-being based on creating Optimal Health. The transformation starts with taking that first step and choosing to take charge of your health for the long term. Reaching a healthy weight is just the beginning.

Unique to our program are three components that provide the foundation and then long-term support that will help you all along the way:

> --Your Free Health Coach
> --The 5 & 1 Plan
> --The Habits of Health System

Your Own Free Health Coach

Caring, knowledgeable, one-on-one support is yours from the first step of your journey toward Optimal Health. With the help of your Health Coach, you'll learn how to internalize the Habits of Health, which are essential to healthy weight maintenance and stress-free living. Your health coach will be your guide and your mentor. Many of our Health Coaches have stood where you stand today and are committed to helping you reach your goals. They lead you toward healthy habits and mentor you in the best ways to overcome your challenges. They are your cheerleaders and your motivators.

Your Health Coach is your guide to a healthier you.

THE 5 & 1 PLAN

Can you eat every 2-3 hours? The 5 & 1 Plan is as simple as choosing five meal replacements and having one Lean & Green Meal daily. Take Shape For Life is fueled by meal replacements recommended by more than 20,000 doctors since 1980 and are clinically proven safe and effective for weight loss.

Each medically formulated meal replacement is individually portioned, calorie and carbohydrate-controlled, and low in fat. Each provides approximately the same nutritional footprint, so you get the vitamins, minerals, and nutrients your body needs when you combine those five Meals with a Lean and Green Meal.

Medically Formulated Meals

You can choose five Meals each day from over 70 different delicious choices, including shakes, soups, stews, chili, oatmeal, eggs, fruit drinks, iced and hot beverages, bars, pancakes, brownies, and puddings.

Lean & Green Meal

Enjoy a meal of lean protein and non-starchy vegetables once a day at whichever time works best for you. Prepare it yourself, grab it on the go, or enjoy it in a restaurant, as long as it follows Lean & Green Meal guidelines.

SUPPORT IS THE KEY TO SUCCESS

The caring support of those around you can be crucial to successful weight loss and maintenance. That's one of the things that makes Take Shape For Life so effective.

Our clients are surrounded by a Bio-Network of Support, which includes all the tools you need to succeed from the comfort of your home. It starts with a free Health Coach, but you also benefit from:

--An online community full of program information, recipes, and more
--Doctors' support calls
--Nurses' support calls
--Habits of Health maintenance calls
--Nutritional support
--Social Media connections
--Dr. A's Habits of Health

With us as your guide, using Dr. A's Habits of Health System is your guide to living a longer, healthier life. It helps you learn how to make small, consistent changes in everything from your diet to your attitude so you can learn how to achieve lasting results that can lead to a lifetime of Optimal Health. The path is clear.

Take the first step in your journey with Take Shape For Life today by giving us a call at (623) 377-9020, or email us at info@coachingyoutohealth.com

Patch Up For Life!

HAVE YOU BEEN PATCHED YET?

What if you could experience a level of health and vitality that you have not experienced since you were in your youth?

In golf we often say "Hit 'em long and finish strong" When it comes to our health, we want our minds, body and spirit to be fully charged so we can "Live Long and Live Strong."

The future of our wellness is in Regenerative Medicine. Knowing the latest research and published studies, such as "How to harness the power of light through a new wearable patch technology," Adults and athletes are experiencing a new level of mental clarity, energy, strength, stamina, restful sleep, and beyond. More information is at Thisisitinfo.com.

Keep learning to look your best, do your best and be your best. If you don't know what you don't know, you can't do what you must. The choices are yours. It's much like the game show years ago, "Truth or Consequences."

Be willing to identify, plan, and execute changes that will allow you to live your best life at any age without limits.

We all have our whys for the decisions we make in life. Often our careers result from a family situation or someone we meet that plants the seed of what we decide to do in life. There are often many seasons of life in our journey to what we do today.

Four car accidents in my early twenties left me searching years later for alternative ways to recover from years of personal health challenges. At age 54, I transitioned from the field of Radiology to focus on encouraging others to be proactive and intentional about their health naturally.

That's why I often wear a "What If" button.

What if there's a better way? What if you can change your life?
Thanks to the many years of being a wife and mom of four children and grandchildren; at 80, I continue to teach what I believe, what I have experienced and what I live.

To Your Health,

Sandie Sopko, RT
Independent LifeWave Partner
602-793-1007
LifeWave.com/Sopko
Thisisitinfo.com

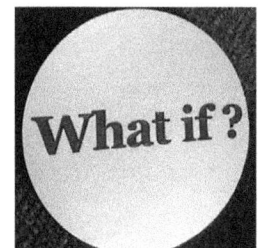

Need a Speaker? Complimentary Community Outreach
--Water - How It Can Change Your Life!
--Truth or Consequences - The Choice Is Yours!
--The Power of Light Technology

Book Recommendations

These are books that have helped me in my life. Hope you enjoy and learn from them, also.

—Tom Loegering

The Bible – The operating manual for human beings created by The Manufacturer.

Think and Grow Rich - Napoleon Hill

Master Key to Riches – Napoleon Hill

The Income Investor - George R. Sealy

The Richest Man in Babylon – George S. Clason

Rhinoceros Success – Scott Alexander

Atlas Shrugged – Ayn Rand

Rich Dad, Poor Dad – Robert Kiyosaki

The Good Profit – Charles Koch

Biofeedback: An Introduction For Consumers – David Phelan Dr.

A's Habits of Health – Dr. Wayne Andersen

If I Only Had a Mulligan - Kent Chase

Jesus Is My Mulligan - Kent Chase

Who Moved My Cheese - Spencer Johnson MD

Other Financial Considerations

Your Credit Rating – Keeping Score

As you complete your business plan and prepare to acquire the success you have earned, you need these eight ways to raise and then protect your credit score.

If you are average, you have 3-4 credit cards and 3-4 installment loans, like a mortgage, car loan, student loans, and personal loans. How you use your credit cards will reflect on your credit score, and your credit score will govern the interest rates you pay, or, in some cases, whether you get a loan or not.

Here are eight ways to use and protect your credit score.

1. Get a free credit report for yourself each year—contact www.annualcreditreport.com.

2. Learn to read your credit report. Check for missing items or incorrect information. Fix errors immediately. The error could be identity theft. Check www.ftc.gov. You need a FICO score above 720 to get good loans and rates. A minimum of 630 or higher will get you a better loan.

3. Pay your bills on time. This is a major way to improve your score while you save late fees, which can lead to bad marks on your credit report that last seven years.

4. Don't move credit card balances from card to card; doing so will result in higher balances, which will lower your score.

5. Don't close accounts for no reason. As your available credit decreases, your score will also decline. Credit agencies like to see an established history of using your credit well.

6. You have a business plan. Make sure you make a monthly cash flow projection. If you spend more than you earn and put it on the cards, you must alter your spending or increase your income.

7. Contact your credit card companies and ask to have your interest rates lowered. If you get no response, pay that card down and keep it with a minimum balance for several months, then call and make the same request. It does work. Ask, and you can receive!

8. Finally, know you can repair past lousy credit, but you must take charge of your spending habits and protect your credit score. You must start using credit as an asset rather than a liability. Take action now, improving your score will become in- creasingly difficult over time. Be careful of using companies that promise to fix your bad credit history, some do not do as they promise and can further damage your credit.

How to Qualify For and Get a Loan

Getting a loan can seem overwhelming, especially if you've never had one or had a bad experience before. This guide will help you understand the process and prepare for success.

1. Be Ready to Tell Your Story

Lenders want to know why you need the loan and how you plan to use it. A business plan can help explain your goals and strategy.

2. Explain Your Team

If you are borrowing for a business, lenders want to know who is involved and their roles. Strong management gives them confidence in your success.

3. Know How Much You Need & How You Will Pay It Back

      --Calculate the exact amount you need.
      --Plan how you will repay the loan (your projected income should cover at least 1.25 times the loan payment).
      --Be ready to offer collateral (something valuable like property or equipment the lender can take if you don't repay).

4. Check Your Finances

      --Keep good financial records with a bookkeeper or accounting system.
      --Review your credit report—many credit scores contain errors that can hurt your chances of approval.

5. Understand Your Cash Flow

Lenders will look at your past cash flow (money coming in and out) over 12, 24, or 36 months. Be ready to show:

      --The most likely financial outcome.
      --A worst-case scenario.
      --A best-case scenario.

6. Plan for Future Expenses

      --List the equipment or assets you need for the next 1-3 years.
      --Plan for routine and unexpected costs.
      --Show how you will use the loan money and contribute to the business financially.

7. Know Your Debts

      --Keep your debts (including mortgage payments) below 38% of your income.
      --Be honest about what you owe.

8. Gather Required Documents

You will need:

>--Three years of tax returns.
>--A completed loan application.

>--A list of all debts you owe.
>--A personal financial statement (if applicable, with a trust as a guarantee).

9. Be Aware of Red Flags

These factors may hurt your chances of getting approved:

>--Bankruptcy (especially Chapter 7).
>--Liens (legal claims against your property).
>--Pending lawsuits.

10. Prepare for the Meeting

>--Be professional and ready to answer questions.
>--Bring key team members who help manage the business.
>--Allow enough time to discuss details with the lender.

What Lenders Look For

CHARACTER: Your credit score shows your willingness to repay.

>--Below 640 = unlikely to get approved.
>--640-680 = difficult but possible.
>--680-720 = better chances.
>--720+ = strong approval odds.
>--Any legal issues can also impact your approval chances.

CAPACITY: Lenders want proof that your income can cover loan payments.

>--You usually need three years of tax returns.
>--Your latest tax return is the most important.
>--Your cash flow should cover at least 1.25 times your loan payments.

CAPITAL: How much money have you invested?

>--A lender prefers a debt-to-capital ratio of no more than 4:1.
>--Example: If you need a $200,000 loan, you should have at least $60,000 in cash and assets.

CONDITION: Your business type and the economy matter.

>--Some industries (like restaurants) are high-risk and more challenging to get loans for.
>--Economic conditions (like a recession) can also affect approval.

COLLATERAL: What assets can secure the loan?

> --SBA loans may not require much collateral.
> --Bank loans focus more on your cash flow than assets.

By preparing in advance and understanding what lenders look for, you can improve your chances of getting the loan you need. Success or failure—the choice is yours!

Additional Tips for Growing Your Wealth to $1 Million

Achieving financial independence and growing your wealth to $1 million requires discipline, strategy, and time. Here are some key steps to help you reach that goal.

Eliminate Obstacles
Before prioritizing retirement savings, tackle high-interest debt like credit cards. Paying off these debts frees up money that would otherwise be lost to high interest rates. Next, an emergency fund should be built to prevent the need for costly early withdrawals from retirement accounts in case of financial setbacks.

Start Now
The sooner you begin saving for retirement, the more time your money has to grow. If your employer offers a 401(k) or another retirement plan, enroll immediately and contribute regularly—especially if there's an employer match, which is essentially free money. No employer plan? Open a solo 401(k) or an IRA to start investing.

Consistent contributions are key to reaching $1 million by retirement. Assuming an 8% return, contributing early and often will maximize your growth.

Increase Contributions Over Time
If saving feels difficult, start small and aim to increase contributions annually.

Here's how:

> --Boost Your Income – Seek pay raises, promotions, side hustles, or job changes that increase earnings. Investing in continuing education can also lead to higher income and net worth.
>
> --Reduce Expenses – When you pay off a debt, redirect that money into your retirement account. For example, if a $250 monthly car payment ends, add that amount to your 401(k) contribution.
>
> --Max Out Contributions – In 2025, the maximum 401(k) contribution is $23,500 for those under 50 and $30,500 for those 50 and older. Strive to contribute as much as possible to maximize tax advantages and compound growth.

Roll Over Old Accounts
When changing jobs, don't leave your retirement savings behind. Roll over old 401(k) plans into a new employer's or IRA plan. Doing so can reduce fees, consolidate accounts, and ensure continuous contributions to your future wealth.

Invest in Property
While retirement accounts are the primary wealth-building tool for most, homeownership is another key driver of financial success. A home can appreciate over time, adding to your net worth. If you're not a homeowner, explore first-time home- buyer programs offering down payment assistance to help you get started.

By eliminating obstacles, starting early, increasing contributions, consolidating accounts, and investing in property, you'll reach $1 million in wealth and secure financial independence.

Protection – Nine Steps to Protect Against Identity Theft

1. When in doubt, SHRED. People are arrested every day for diving into our trash for personal information. Shredding works.

2. Don't provide more personal information than the transaction demands. While you might provide all your information on a mortgage application, you should not provide the same amount of information for an ordinary retail purchase.

3. Ask the merchant how they will protect the information they are asking for. Be comfortable with them protecting your information.

4. Your Social Security number (SSN) is required by law only for transactions involving federal taxes. Please don't give your SSN to everybody who asks for it.

5. Always ask for alternative personal identification on driver's licenses and other documents. Randomly assigned numbers offer the best protection.

6. Instead of signing your credit and debit cards write, "Ask for ID." Then thank the clerk for protecting your identity.

7. Retrieve your mail from the mailbox as soon as you can. ID thieves will follow the delivery person and steal the mail, immediately.

8. Ladies, you are a target when you leave your purse in the shopping cart unsecured. Use the child's strap to secure your wallet.

9. When using the Internet, the address browser will start with "http:" This means the world can see what you are doing. If you are using personal information, make sure the address changes to "https:" This tells you that the site uses 128-bit encryption and that your session is unlikely to be hacked.

Appendix H

GPS Champions Club

Change a Child's Life for Just $24/Month – Join the GPS Champions Club

What if just **$24 a month** could help change the course of a child's life?

At **Golf Program in Schools (GPS)**, we believe golf is more than a game, it's a gateway to a life of purpose. Through our in-school program, we teach **Courtesy, Respect, Honesty, and Integrity** while helping K–12 P/E students build confidence, character, and career direction.

By becoming a monthly member of the **GPS Champions Club**, you'll sponsor a child in need each month and guide them along their **PATH** to success:

- **Persistence**: "If at first you don't succeed, try, try again." Golf embodies how practice can be and is a powerful tool.
- **Achievement**: Students gain increased confidence in their abilities with positive input and direction.
- **Trustworthiness**: "If it is to be, it is up to me." Golfers keep their own score, developing trust and respect in themselves and other players.
- **Healthy** Lifestyle: A lifestyle incorporating golf is a great way to have fun and enjoy fresh air and regular exercise without the need for exceptional athletic abilities.
    Sponsor a student: $24/month introduces one child to the program every month.
    Sponsor a Class: $600 provides golf lessons to an entire class.
    Sponsor a School: $6,000 provides life lessons for the entire school
    Corporate Sponsorships: Partner with GPS to make a lasting impact and gain brand visibility.

What you'll provide:

    Free golf instruction to students during school hours
    Life lessons rooted in strong core values
    Opportunities for scholarships and careers in golf
    Support for programs for veterans, domestic violence survivors, and underserved youth

You'll receive annual impact stories and invitations to our events.
You can even gift your membership in honor of someone who believes in giving kids a better future.

Join the GPS Champions Club today at www.golfps.org.

Together we can guide the next generation—on the course, in the classroom, and into a stronger future.

Warm regards,
Tom Loegering
Founder & CEO
Golf Program in Schools, Inc.
www.golfps.org

The next step in your financial progress. . .

The Income Investor

Give Yourself a Raise Every Month

George R. Sealy

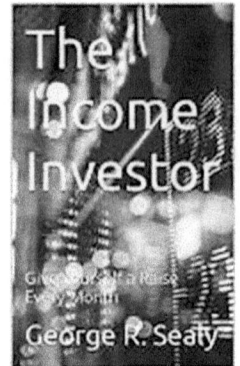

What the book is about. . .

The Income Investor strives to help people create a solid, reliable, growing income stream. It presents processes that have worked successfully for decades. It is relevant for young investors who want to get started on a long life of income production. It is also relevant for seniors who want to augment Social Security and pension income.

The book begins with the concept that an income investor must adopt the proper mindset. The first rule is that people must take responsibility for their financial future. No one else will be as concerned. The second rule is that adopting a repeatable process will lead to ultimate success.

The book continues by outlining the tools necessary for income investing. This is followed by definitions of financial terms that novice investors can understand. The difference between income creation and wealth building is emphasized.

The middle portion of the book discusses savings accounts, Certificates of Deposit, and stock dividends. Each has a role to play. Most of the text concerns stock dividends. It describes screening criteria and processes based on the most fundamental and critical elements of corporate finance. Income growth is highlighted. Goal setting is considered a critical factor to ultimate success.

The last section of the book provides a step-by-step game plan to get started. It talks about how to handle adversity. Appendices provide additional information on specific topics.

Solid concepts for success. . .

✓ Being responsible for one's financial future
✓ Having a process mindset
✓ Understanding income investing versus wealth building
✓ Knowing financial terms
✓ Knowing the tools you need
✓ Knowing income alternatives and their roles
✓ Tracking progress
✓ Setting goals
✓ Handling adversity

The Income Investor is available on Amazon in soft cover and Kindle formats.

Start giving yourself a raise today!

PEOPLE WHO FOUND
SUCCESS
DESPITE
FAILURES

J.K. Rowling was rejected by
TWELVE
Publishers before
Harry Potter and
The Philosopher's Stone
was accepted!

Walt Disney was
turned down
302 times
before he got
financing for creating
Disneyland!

Tom,

Thank you so much for all of your help. Also a big thanks for your book

"Success or Failure The Choice is yours!

Great book! On page 11 "understand that YOU are the business you are operating", really stuk with m ... our book is an amazing resource, and I love how helpful it is Thank you once again Tom!

Sincerely

Ethen G Putnam

www.ingramcontent.com/pod-product-compliance
Lightning Source LLC
Chambersburg PA
CBHW081823200326
41597CB00023B/4368